MOON SIGNS

MOON SIGNS

YOUR LUNAR ASTROLOGICAL GUIDE

Marion Williamson

SIRIUS

All images courtesy of Shutterstock.

SIRIUS

This edition published in 2023 by Sirius Publishing, a division of
Arcturus Publishing Limited,
26/27 Bickels Yard, 151–153 Bermondsey Street,
London SE1 3HA

ISBN: 978-1-3988-3054-7
AD008859UK

Printed in China

CONTENTS

INTRODUCTION

WHAT IS A MOON SIGN?

What's your sign? You know by heart whether you're a feisty Aries, a serene Taurus or an outgoing Leo, but your 'sign' only refers to your Sun sign, the section of the zodiac the Sun was travelling through on the day you were born. Sun signs describe your outer personality traits and core identity — the side of you that you're happy to beam out to the world.

You also have a Moon sign, which is the zodiac sign the Moon was found in at the time of your birth. In astrology, your Moon sign describes who you are on an emotional level. Your Moon shines a profoundly insightful light on a much deeper lever of your psyche — which makes it far sexier and more mysterious than your Sun sign, which illuminates the characteristics everyone can see.

WHAT DOES YOUR MOON SIGN REVEAL?

Your Moon sign is your private self and represents your ever-changing emotions and how they feel in your body. Your intuitive responses, moods, longings, fears and motivation are all expressed by where the Moon was at your time of birth. It's your essence — who you are on the inside, beneath your socially acceptable Sun sign. If you want to know yourself well, or are compelled to understand the people around you, the Moon offers a swell of dynamic psychological insight that unlocks the door to the authentic person within.

Understanding your Moon sign gives you the tools to master your fears and better control how you respond when you feel triggered. You'll understand what attracts you in love, look your vulnerabilities in the eye, and appreciate why you act in a particular way to protect or defend yourself.

The Moon's fluctuating phases and fast-moving nature reflect your dynamic inner landscape, pushing and pulling on your emotions, just as it does with the ocean's tides.

COMBINING YOUR SUN AND MOON SIGNS

In astrology, the Sun represents the light of your consciousness. It's your creative self, who you appear to be in the public eye, and the expression of the identity you're most comfortable with. Your Moon is your subconscious — the feelings, fears and attractions that drive you from below the surface. When you merge your Sun and Moon sign positions, you have a cosmic marriage, a synthesis between your light and dark sides — what you're open about and what you keep secret.

When you know your Moon sign, you'll work out why you never felt like you were a one hundred percent work-obsessed Capricorn, or a theatrical, outgoing Leo. That's because the traits associated with your Moon will alter your Sun sign characteristics — blending, strengthening and even clashing with them. There's a section in this book on combining your Sun and Moon signs at the end of each Moon sign chapter.

HOW DO I FIND MY MOON SIGN?

While the Sun takes a year to move through each of the 12 zodiac signs (that's why a year is 12 months long), the Moon only takes 2.5 days. Its position changes so quickly that the best way to locate where your Moon was at your birth is to look up your astrological birth chart. You can find a free copy of your unique map of the heavens at www.astro.com.

Click the Free Horoscopes link, then tap Charts & Data, and finally Chart Drawing & Ascendant. Input your date, time and place of birth, then click on your chart. Now find the crescent Moon symbol within the circular map. The segment that contains your Moon will have the symbol of the zodiac sign on the outer edge of the circle — this is your Moon sign. You can also locate the crescent Moon symbol in the table on the left-hand side of the chart. This will have the abbreviated names of the zodiac sign next to it. The Moon changes sign every 2.5 days, so on some days it will move from one zodiac sign to the next, which can occur at any time of day — that's why it's important that you have as accurate a birth time as possible.

DON'T KNOW YOUR TIME OF BIRTH?

If you don't know the exact time, look at the chart and see if the Moon was in the same zodiac sign all day by changing your time of birth by a few hours. It might not have changed signs. But if it did, read the description for the two signs the Moon was in that day, and you'll usually have a strong feeling about which one you are. Remember, you're looking for the sign that describes your deepest feelings, instincts, fears and longings.

MOON

IN

ARIES

YOUR FIRST INSTINCTS

Do something!

Your default position when facing a challenge or experiencing sudden, strong feelings is to act — and fast. Your legendary passion and enthusiasm are impossible to subdue, and the fiery momentum of your feelings propels you into physical action. Your instinct is to take control and make something happen — anything — otherwise you'll become unbearably impatient and your temper will rocket. Your leadership skills come into their own when you're facing a crisis, and you feel more confident when you're the one calling the shots. Waiting for others to make a move drives you nuts, and you genuinely believe that your way is the best for everyone involved, whether you're hosting a fancy-dress party or arranging a funeral.

Impulsive and fearless

Your responses are impulsive, spontaneous and disarmingly honest — and you bravely wear your heart on your sleeve for everyone to see. You're proud that you have nothing to hide, and there's a childlike purity to your emotional impulses. Not one to dwell too long on sad or uneasy feelings, you prefer to pull your metaphorical socks up and soldier gamely on, with complete faith that you'll cope with whatever life throws at you. One of your most endearing qualities is that although you do have a legendary temper — and won't hold back if someone has offended or hurt you — you forgive and forget just as fast as you got upset, and rarely hold a grudge.

WHAT YOU'RE ATTRACTED TO IN OTHERS

Confidence

A wildly independent person, you need someone in your life who respects that you need to make your own decisions, but you also don't want a partner who'll let you get your own way all the time. Because you're so used to fighting for what you want, you can be a little self-centred at times, so having someone who is strong enough to challenge your decisions can be refreshing. You'd enjoy a partner who can see past your ballsy bossiness and understand that sometimes you're just fronting stuff out to protect your real feelings. People who have overcome personal difficulties or have a heroic story to tell will inspire you and captivate your heart. You want to feel proud of your other half, and you love when you feel like the pair of you are the stars in your own adventure.

Balanced judgment

You're in awe of people who take time to make decisions, because you're the opposite — you charge in passionately with strong opinions, and to hell with the consequences. Patient, thoughtful types with graceful social skills make you realize you have some refining to do, and you admire the effort they put into making other people happy. You can be a little rough around the edges with people because you expect them to resist or disagree with you. The peacemakers of the world intrigue you, and you'll discover through them that cooperating with others and taking a more nuanced approach in relationships can get you what you want without rubbing people up the wrong way.

YOUR FEARS AND EMOTIONAL RESPONSES

Don't lie to me

Honesty is your superpower, so to have it used against you can leave you feeling bewildered. You're suspicious of anyone who takes too long to tell you how they feel because you suspect that any kind of overthinking could be a sign that they're making up a story. You have no guile — what you see is what you get. So when you sense someone is hatching a plan, your Spidey senses tingle and you put up a wall. Your disarming honesty encourages your friends and loved ones be open with you in return. When they're hesitant or reserved, you get nervous that they're hiding things from you. Having a little more faith in others' motivations might help you relax, as not everyone is as brave or confident as you when expressing exactly what's going on in their heart.

Sharing makes you nervous

You have learned to look after yourself first, and you know that if you want something you have to go out into the world and fight for it. Perhaps in your past you felt let down by a caregiver and were left feeling vulnerable. Maybe you learned the hard way that being dependent on people made you feel helpless, and vowed you'd never be in that situation again. Losing your independence or being overly reliant on a partner is a chilling prospect, so you might overcompensate by fiercely being your own person. Your defiant self-belief and confidence can make your loved ones back off a little, as they think you don't need them. But sometimes it's the toughest people who have the most fragile hearts.

WHAT YOU KEEP SECRET

Hopeless romantic

Behind all your impressive, fiery bravado you're a hopeless romantic. Aries is the first sign of the zodiac — the baby — and when your Moon sign is placed here there's a child's purity and innocence to your emotional temperament. You love with an uncomplicated fervour that is simple and strong, and you give your heart completely. You're an exciting person to be in a relationship with — flirtatious, passionate, sexy and daring. You fight for the people you care about and delight in the intensity of your feelings. Your trust and confidence are hard won, which is why it hurts so much if it doesn't work out.

Protective shield

You guard your heart gallantly and have discovered that the bigger the noise you make, and the bolder your claims, the less people probe the chinks in your armour. Your bravado and self-sufficiency are a cunning disguise, protecting you from relying too heavily on anyone else. Your instincts are fast and sharp, so if you feel the slightest hint that someone is growing cold on you, you'll get in there first and end the relationship before they've had a chance to consciously think it through. If someone does break your heart, your pain is real and raw, but because you are able to express yourself so sincerely, you are able to process your emotions more quickly than the other zodiac signs. Phew!

Sun and Moon combinations

Aries Moon with **Aries Sun**

Look out, world — here you come! You're the personality equivalent of an Olympic gold medal. You set out to win and you lead in all you do, though underneath your confident exterior you're as romantic as an eighteenth century bodice-ripper. Your fiercely independent nature can scare some people off, but that's only because you're protecting yourself from getting hurt.

Aries Moon with **Taurus Sun**

On the surface you're cool and calm, thorough and patient. You dislike being pushed for answers, and the more rushed you feel, the further you dig in your heels. You're a mystery to people who don't know you well because they can sense there's something simmering beneath your unflappable layers.

Aries Moon with **Gemini Sun**

Your decisive, passionate, emotional side is tempered by your flexible, restless Gemini Sun. You're deeply passionate and brave, but your nimble, changeable Sun keeps you open to different points of view. Playful and curious, you're an impulsive, light-hearted entertainer who is never gloomy for long.

Aries Moon with **Cancer Sun**

Your quick, impulsive emotions are close to the surface. Your sensitive Cancer Sun and fiery feelings make you a reactive but deeply caring person. You are very protective and worry about your loved ones, but over time you'll learn to give yourself space before jumping to conclusions.

Aries Moon with **Leo Sun**

The world knows exactly what you think and feel because your Leo personality is not shy, and your Aries emotions are loud and true. There's no holding you back when you decide to do something, and you want to throw yourself into all the fabulous experiences life has to offer.

Aries Moon with **Virgo Sun**

Under your organized, practical personality you're an impulsive, fun-loving soul. Methodical and tenacious, you're unstoppably determined, and you love to surprise people who may underestimate your shy exterior. You're more easily hurt than you'd ever admit, but you'll show your claws if anyone tries to push you around.

Aries Moon with **Libra Sun**

You're always balancing how you really feel with what seems socially appropriate. Relationships are very important to you, and you hate it when you're not on good terms with people, but it's tricky to keep calm

when your emotions are white hot. You crackle with magnetic allure.

Aries Moon with **Scorpio Sun**

With a mischievous glint in your eye, your secretive Scorpio nature means it's your instinct not to reveal too much about your true feelings. But when you trust someone, they'll see what an intense, driven person you truly are, and hopefully they'll be more awestruck than intimidated!

Aries Moon with **Sagittarius Sun**

Adventure-loving, broad-minded and enthusiastic, you have a can-do attitude and your pioneering soul longs for travel and excitement. You dive in where angels fear to tread, but can sometimes lose interest when your fiery nature is dampened by red tape or practicalities. But you're never daunted for long; you learn fast and perfect your skills for next time.

Aries Moon with **Capricorn Sun**

You're an ambitious, goal-oriented character, and you have likely tamed your impulsive side or learned to slow down and control your live-fast-die-young side. Your Aries Moon makes you competitive, and your Capricorn Sun gives you the quiet confidence to reach the highest summits. Nobody else stands a chance when you're in the race.

Aries Moon with **Aquarius Sun**

Your full-on, reactive responses can be at odds with your aloof, scientific-minded Aquarius Sun. You might feel a little detached sometimes, then surprise yourself with how hotly you can argue or how totally you can fall in love. When you're feeling balanced, you're an amazing campaigner and champion for human rights.

Aries Moon with **Pisces Sun**

Poetic and dreamy, compassionate and reclusive, your gentle Pisces Sun is at odds with your strong, independent, firecracker Moon. When you're firing on all cylinders, your decisive Aries side gives you direction, and your insightful Pisces Sun softens your quick impulses and makes you want to share your experiences.

MOON
IN
TAURUS

YOUR FIRST INSTINCTS

Don't rock the boat

As a security-conscious, comfort-loving Taurus Moon, your gut feeling in any new situation is to keep things calm and safe, and to proceed with caution. Whether you're in the middle of a chaotic family drama, you've spent the day dealing with angry customers or you think you're falling in love with your sister's boyfriend, your first reaction is to take a deep breath, get into your flannel PJs, fix yourself an indulgent hot chocolate, then think how best to do as little as possible. Your placid nature needs stability and sustenance — you'd never make a dramatic scene that would draw unnecessary attention or drain your energy. As with your bank balance, treasured possessions and precious friendships, you like to conserve your strength so it's there when you really need it.

Comfortable and familiar

You're soothed by comfort, beauty and quality craftsmanship, and seek solace in the tangible world. When you need to make a tough decision, or you feel emotionally drained, a pleasant and restful environment is essential. You can't make emotional decisions in a dirty, loud or busy place; you need home comforts and familiar surroundings to make you feel safe. You hang on to the things you love, and that includes old friends who know you well. A sensible chat with a well-loved pal will help you feel grounded and will encourage you to act if necessary. You're no fan of change, and it can take an age to make up your mind. But when you do you, you're one of the most quietly strong-willed people on the planet.

WHAT YOU'RE ATTRACTED TO IN OTHERS

Cool in a crisis

You don't waste energy going after people you're attracted to, but you're blessed with an irresistible magnetic power that draws people you're interested in into your orbit. You'll give your right arm to avoid emotionally messy or confrontational situations, so when you see someone who is staying level-headed when everyone else is going bananas, it's hard to disguise your admiration. You do your best to avoid challenging situations, so watching someone adeptly master a challenging situation is your idea of sexy. People who are quietly persistent — patient teachers, cool driving instructors or stressed parents being kind to tantrum-prone children — earn your profound respect. One of the quickest and simplest ways to capture your heart is through your stomach. If you discover someone's as passionate about food and cooking as you are, you're hooked.

Loyal and trustworthy

You don't dive into new situations, and you're suspicious of anyone who decides you're the love of their life before getting to you know you well. Spontaneous gestures of love just freak you out, so when someone takes the time to wine and dine you, and asks plenty of questions, you find them hard to resist. Because trust is so important to you, it can take you an age to decide on the right person, but when you make up your mind it's usually for life. You commit to your partner like you do anything: wholly and completely. Your idea of hot might be a little on the tepid side for some, but sensible, well-mannered people who are good with money and dress well definitely have your vote.

YOUR FEARS AND EMOTIONAL RESPONSES

Losing it

Your reason for living is to build, grow and conserve, and losing what you have worked hard to acquire is your greatest fear. Once something has been in your possession for a while, you get attached. You only lend to people you can trust to return your money or possessions, and you guard your treasures jealously. If you feel insecure in a relationship, you cling to the people you care about, which can cause them to move even further away. Letting people go is your hardest lesson, but when you show your trust in them, they'll happily return your love. Losing your composure or control is another cause of anxiety, as no doubt you've felt hugely uncomfortable when others have witnessed one of your legendary, but rare, emotional outbursts.

Never change

You'll stubbornly argue that black is white if you feel you're being undermined or fear that you could lose something or someone you value. Defending yourself against hurt by refusing to acknowledge that things have changed doesn't help you evolve. Instead, you dig yourself in deeper and refuse to budge, even though it's clear that everyone around you is adapting and moving on. Change is harder for you than most because it takes you such a long time to get used to things; more than once you'll have experienced the rug being pulled from your feet, just as you were getting comfortable. Much of the beauty of your personality lies in your resilience and determination, and you can use those same skills to help you cope with life's surprises.

WHAT YOU KEEP SECRET

Silent but violent

What you and only a few very close loved ones know is that although you're probably the most patient and serene person in the zodiac, when you blow your top, it's devastating. Perhaps you have yet to experience your own anger; after all, it's possibly a twice- or maybe thrice-in-a-lifetime occurrence. When you see red, it's rarely spontaneous — though it may look like that to outsiders — but there will have been a slow drip, drip effect or something that's ground you down for years until you finally flip your lid. Your rage could be caused by anything from your brother-in-law's continual disrespect of your time or possessions to the built-up frustration of a nagging neck pain. When the final straw floats past your eyes, you see red and utterly forget yourself. Your outrage is jaw-droppingly destructive and, actually, kind of awesome.

Passion for pleasure

Another thing you keep to yourself is that you'd sell the family silver for a back rub. You're a profoundly sensual being and you take pleasure seriously, whether that's food, sex or expensive cocktails at a fashionable jazz club. A proud and knowledgeable gourmet, you might be obsessed with French patisserie or heavenly single-origin coffee. Or you might be a master chocolatier on the quiet. You're a serious music fan and could easily part with an eye-watering amount of hard-earned cash on records, concerts or musicals. You turn a blind eye to the expense because to you, it's as vital as oxygen. Divine perfume or sumptuous grooming products can also hypnotize you with their beautiful aromas and luxurious packaging. Your smouldering sensuality of course extends into the bedroom, and anyone lucky enough to have spent a night of passion with you is probably still a little giddy.

Sun and Moon combinations

Taurus Moon with **Aries Sun**

You're dynamic and energetic, a decisive leader, and always ready to spring into action. To the outside world you're confident, brave and tough, but emotionally you're much calmer and more thoughtful than others first realize. Deeply loyal and sensual, you have an eye for beauty and are a born romantic.

Taurus Moon with **Taurus Sun**

Infinitely reliable and sensible, you prefer tried-and-tested routes and find comfort in familiar people, surroundings and routines. You're patient and serene, and stick with what and whom you know; but if your patience is tested, once in a while you can spectacularly blow your top. Spontaneity unsettles you unless there's food or a massage involved.

Taurus Moon with **Gemini Sun**

Gemini Suns usually find it difficult to concentrate on one thing at a time, but your stable Taurus Moon keeps you focused and reliable. You're on a constant quest to better yourself, and you're a walking, talking Wikipedia who loves to exchange information. You love talking to people, plants, pets and — if there's nobody else around — yourself.

Taurus Moon with **Cancer Sun**

Emotionally intelligent and sensitive, you form long-lasting, meaningful bonds with others. Financially shrewd and tenacious, with an astonishingly good memory, your Cancer Sun makes you shy but very protective of the people you love. Your food-loving Taurus Moon blends well with your nurturing Cancer Sun, and you're probably an excellent chef or gardener.

Taurus Moon with **Leo Sun**

Confident, trustworthy and dramatic, your flamboyant, attention-seeking Sun is at odds with your quieter, more practical emotional side. You might be an impulsive spender and thrive in the limelight, but emotionally, once you've made up your mind about someone, you rarely change it. Thoughtful and considerate, you're cautious about who you give your heart to.

Taurus Moon with **Virgo Sun**

Practical, resilient and focused, you tackle challenges methodically. You have an analytical mind and brilliant research skills that help you quickly grasp facts and figures. Kind and logical, you can always see a down-to-earth solution, and your friends love you for it. You are stoical and composed; it takes a serious drama to ruffle your feathers.

Taurus Moon with **Libra Sun**

You're a diplomatic soul who works hard to get along with everyone, and you're often the peacemaker in your friend group. Your heightened sense of fairness and balance means you have an eye for beauty and design. You like to look good, and enjoy spending money on clothes, home furnishings and beautiful objects.

Taurus Moon with **Scorpio Sun**

You're dynamic and sexy, an intense person with amazing stamina and willpower. You have a quiet confidence in your abilities, and rarely need to shout about them.

You dislike change, need a routine, and hate to be rushed. If loved ones get impatient, you just dig in your heels and refuse to budge.

Taurus Moon with **Sagittarius Sun**

To most people, you are optimistic, spontaneous and adventurous; but the people who know you best see a more considerate, practical side to your personality. Although you love a challenge, you're not a risk taker — especially when it comes to your feelings. You're generous and outspoken, loyal and trustworthy.

Taurus Moon with **Capricorn Sun**

Emotionally grounded, with a dry sense of humour, you approach life methodically as a series of goals and ambitions. Feeling secure is vital for you to thrive, so you're likely a saver more than a spender, and prefer traditional values over anything too radical. You're not a fan of surprises,

but you tickle others with your hilarious dry wit.

Taurus Moon with **Aquarius Sun**

Cool-headed but unpredictable, you're an enigma to people who don't know you. A clever mix of Aquarian eccentricity and genius with a solid, dependable core, you're emotionally grounded but restless, with lightning-fast intelligence. Unique and social, you're a quick learner, but your feelings are solid and unwavering.

Taurus Moon with **Pisces Sun**

Fantastically creative and artistic, you get drawn into daydreams, fantasies and poetry due to your wild imagination. However, your emotional centre is earthy and practical. You might get carried away by your whims and passions, but your sensible Taurus heart keeps your feet planted firmly on the ground.

MOON
IN
GEMINI

YOUR FIRST INSTINCTS

Research and share

You're better prepared than most when life throws you an emotional curveball, and you may even see it as an opportunity to make some positive changes. Your first response in any crisis is to find out as much as possible about what's going on. Emotions are tricky waters for you; you spend so much time in your head that when a strong feeling takes you by surprise, it knocks you sideways. You'll immediately turn to Google and social media, and family and friends will be shaken and sieved for information. It's mind-blowing how much you can digest and memorize in a short space of time, but arming yourself with facts and information makes you feel less vulnerable and gives you a little breathing space from the feelings themselves.

Communicate with fellow humans

Whether you're experiencing anxiety, lust or fear, or are overwhelmed or confused, you'll want to understand and explore what's going on. Talking therapies are right up your alley, as you'll find the psychology incredibly interesting; but remember to keep the sessions focused on you, rather than asking lots of questions about how it all works. Self-help books are another excellent option, as reading is a favourite way for you to relax. Writing down how you feel will also allow you to get to the core of what's troubling you. Viewing your emotions through such an intellectual filter helps you get partway, but to be free of old hurts, you may have to return to the source of the pain and relive it.

WHAT YOU'RE ATTRACTED TO IN OTHERS

Fun-loving and open-minded

You're on the lookout for freedom-loving people who aren't encumbered with heavy emotional baggage, and little turns you off faster than someone who has made up their mind before they know all the facts. So, when you encounter open minds and carefree hearts, you find them easy to like. If they're laid-back and optimistic, all the better to balance your highly strung nerves. You need someone

who's as delighted by whims as you are, who is keen to take a car-mechanic course and learn astrophysics on the side. You can teach each other coding languages and do one another's Tarot cards to keep each other from thinking dark thoughts. After all, Gemini is the sign of the Twins; emotionally, you can switch from your light and airy side to sour and pessimistic without much warning.

Intellectual depth

Your encyclopaedic mind is impressive, and you surprise people with your astonishing knowledge of everything from hieroglyphics to the mating rituals of puffer fish. But every now and then you meet someone with real, deep wisdom, the kind of person who profoundly ponders the mysteries of life and death and lives by their beliefs. Spiritual gurus, life coaches, psychotherapists and priests all have you under their spell. Even the happy homeless guy outside your gym has you spellbound because they've found their focus — an idea, belief or vision that they never grow tired of. You're so caught up in your continually shifting interests and passions that you rarely settle on one subject for long; so when you meet someone who has mastered that stillness and depth, you find it intensely admirable and quite sexy.

YOUR FEARS AND EMOTIONAL RESPONSES

Silence and stillness

You get the fear when relationships get stuck in a predictable pattern, or when you realize you could do your job in your sleep. Stillness and silence are stagnation in your book — the anti-you — something to be avoided at all costs if you want to stay alive. Anything that smacks of long-term commitment, whether that's marriage, mortgage, or watering your neighbour's houseplants while they're on holiday, brings you out in hives. You're not patient enough to wait for slower types to catch up with you, and the thought of having to endure dull, routine tasks in a job for years brings out your split personality, and your evil twin comes out to liven things up a bit.

Looking up your bottom with a microscope

Your inquisitive Gemini Moon makes it hard to relax because your mind is always on at full volume, tap-dancing to show tunes. This inner restlessness makes you prone to worry, and once you get stuck down that wormhole there's no easy way back. Because you're a bit of a hypochondriac, simple health issues can quickly turn into fantasizing about who'll turn up at your funeral. Overthinking and analyzing are your ways of coping with stress, because knowing the answers makes you feel more in control — but of course not everything has an easy solution. You need to know when enough is enough, and realize that no matter how much you nibble and gnaw at your problems, sometimes life is a logic-defying, slippery fish.

WHAT YOU KEEP SECRET

There are no secrets

If someone tells you something interesting, you'll want to share it. Whether you do will depend on how much you like the person who confided in you and how good a story it is. A salacious and entertaining tale is going to bend you to bursting point until you spill the beans. Your loved ones will of course know this about you, and will likely only give you information they don't mind being halfway round the internet by lunchtime… some might even rely on you for it. You may bend and juggle the facts to create a more entertaining story — but you always take others' tales with a pinch of salt, so why shouldn't you ladle it on too?

Dangerous when bored

You don't want people to know that if you've lost interest in something, you'll get provocative just to liven things up again. You can be a little detached emotionally, and because you're often light years ahead of everyone else's thinking, you can find waiting for everyone else to catch up quite tedious. When you're bored, you become extra talkative and animated in conversation, and you'll do your best to pry something gossip-worthy from whoever you're talking to. You're not always the most discreet person when you're on the prowl for mischief, and likely won't think through the consequences unless you get found out.

Sun and Moon combinations

Gemini Moon with **Aries Sun**

You're a whirlwind, not afraid to go after exactly what you want — and you have the charm and flexibility to adapt to tough circumstances. You're a passionate personality with the wit and guile to sell hobnail boots to mermaids. You're cheerful, positive and hard to resist.

Gemini Moon with **Taurus Sun**

Your emotionally adaptable Gemini Moon lends flexibility to your practical Taurus Sun, so you're not as resistant to change. You're chatty and social, but your home life is important and you've probably kept hold of friendships since childhood. A loyal partner, you're romantic and an eternal optimist.

Gemini Moon with **Gemini Sun**

Unpredictable and lively, nobody can guess what you'll get up to next. You need to feel entertained, as you can get bored easily. You're the fastest brain around, but you're probably not keen on settling down as you'll never feel old or sensible enough. An incredible multitasker, you know a little about everything and have incredible general knowledge.

Gemini Moon with **Cancer Sun**

You're shrewd and sensitive, and your Cancer Sun deepens your emotions; you probably have a close family and a love of home. Your bubbly Gemini Moon means you love company and entertaining, and need a partner who makes you laugh and gives you plenty of emotional space. Your mercurial emotions mean that nothing gets you down for long.

Gemini Moon with **Leo Sun**

You're the life and soul of the party who loves being the centre of attention. Social and attention-grabbing, you'll turn cartwheels to make your friends laugh, and your dramatic personality means you'll never be short of admirers. You're not usually someone who enjoys being on their own.

Gemini Moon with **Virgo Sun**

As soon as you popped out of the womb you were Googling what to expect from life. You likely started talking from an early age, and your communication skills are hot. Emotionally level, you don't let your feelings get in the way of logic — which is great for keeping a cool head, but confusing if you've fallen passionately in love.

Gemini Moon with **Libra Sun**

Charismatic and charming, you can talk your way into, or out of, any situation. Reasonable, fair and open-minded, you're a brilliant debater and are never short of a witty quip. Anger and ugliness turn you off, so you'll always find a way to smooth over troubled waters.

Gemini Moon with **Scorpio Sun**

You are emotionally intelligent, and your sharp intuition helps you see past any smokescreen to what's really going on with people. You're open to talking about other people's feelings, but aren't keen on sharing your own. Independent but passionate, you have intense connections with loved ones.

Gemini Moon with **Sagittarius Sun**

Flirtatious and bubbly, you're the gregarious one in the middle of any party, entertaining people and making new pals. You are warm-hearted and gregarious, and your appetite for new experiences is high. You're an independent person who enjoys sharing your adventurous lifestyle.

Gemini Moon with **Capricorn Sun**

You're a clear thinker who enjoys having goals. Your ambitious Capricorn Sun helps keep your Gemini Moon grounded, and gifts you with a practical outlook on life. Emotionally inquisitive, you rarely wear your heart on your sleeve, but people close to you see a kind, thoughtful person.

Gemini Moon with **Aquarius Sun**

Highly strung and brilliant, you need movement and change. Your friends love your rebellious, quirky personality, but getting in too deep romantically can sound alarm bells, as you're a fun, free spirit. Erratic and spontaneous, you're a rule-breaking maverick. Don't make major life decisions before coffee.

Gemini Moon with **Pisces Sun**

Intuitive and gentle, you always find a way to communicate your feelings, even if that's through creative pursuits rather than openly taking about how you feel. You need to surround yourself with positive people, as you easily absorb others' energies and forget where you end and other people begin.

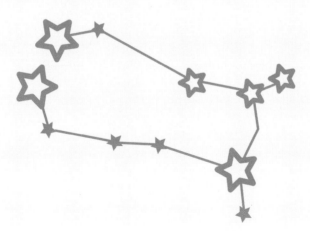

YOUR FIRST INSTINCTS

Am I safe?

Emotions are what you do. Cancer is the most sensitive, emotional sign of the zodiac, and when it's your Moon sign, it magnifies your feelings intensely. You know yourself well, so you'll know that when you first encounter a challenge or an onslaught of feelings, your instinctual reaction is to hunker down in your comfort zone — your protective shell. Your home is your retreat from the outside world, and is where you are completely yourself. Whether your base is a luxury penthouse or a tent in a forest, it's where you let your defences down and can fully relax and feel comfortable with yourself. But when you do feel ready to conquer the outside world, you're quite a tough cookie.

Fiercely protective

Another immediate feeling that's a crucial part of your emotional makeup is to protect your loved ones and belongings. You'll stand in front of tanks if you have to, and can be surprisingly fierce and persistent if you feel that you, your loved ones or your home and possessions are under threat. The love you have for your home and family is the glue that keeps you together, and if that's in jeopardy, you go into overdrive. Overprotective and sometimes fussy, you are the mother of the zodiac, and your heightened nurturing capabilities ensure that every person, pet and houseplant thrives in your care.

WHAT YOU'RE ATTRACTED TO IN OTHERS

Family values

You like strong, responsible people who act like grown-ups — sensible with money, with solid family values. If that person is kind to your mother, they're in. And if they're also a decent cook, you might propose. You're probably looking for a true partner, someone you can raise a family with, who will love and protect them with all their might. You're good with money, so you don't waste time on daydreamers who fritter away their cash or people who don't have a stash saved for a rainy day. You warm to people who like being at home too, as there's nothing more appealing to you than someone you can snuggle up to on the couch for a cosy, romantic evening with some delicious nibbles.

Kindness and commitment

You find commitment a hundred percent sexy. There's no appeal for you in someone who fancies a quick fling, or who's not as excited about domestic bliss as you are. Finding a potential partner who's willing to take things slow, and who takes your feelings seriously, is pure gold. You fall in love quickly, so someone who's not scared of your intensity, and speaks the same language emotionally, is probably in a good position to win your heart. In some ways you're a sweet, old-fashioned romantic who loves to be swept off your feet with candlelit dinners, thoughtful gifts and longing gazes. But when you find that person, you'll be unwaveringly devoted to their happiness for the rest of your life.

YOUR FEARS AND EMOTIONAL RESPONSES

Being exposed

Not a lover of the spotlight, you prefer — metaphorically speaking — to come out of your shell by moonlight. You're quite shy and self-conscious, and sometimes you have troubling dreams about being naked in your local supermarket. You like to have time to get yourself together before meeting people, and if someone turns up at your home unexpectedly, you'll be quite distressed that you haven't had time to hide the dirty dishes or change out of your PJs. Similarly, if you have news, it's not in your nature to just blurt out something rude or painful and risk hurting someone with something they're not prepared for. Even if you're breaking up with your partner or attempting to tell your friend they have terribly bad breath, you'll still not be able to bear their pain or shame and will put a great deal of thought into how you're going to spare their feelings.

Getting hurt

You have a hard shell for a good reason: inside, you're a heartbreakingly gentle soul. Your defensive, tough behaviour is just a smokescreen so that people don't probe further and find out how wounded you are. You disguise your emotional vulnerability by pretending to be resilient, aloof and cool, but the people who know you best love that you're actually none of those. You feel your emotions more intensely than any other Moon sign, which is a wonder to behold if you're happy or excited; but if you're humiliated, sad or hurt, your Cancer Moon needs dignity, comfort and privacy. It's hard for you to forget past hurts, and you invest a good deal of time and effort into avoiding being in that situation again.

WHAT YOU KEEP SECRET

You still have the bus ticket from your first date

Memories are as important as tangible things for you, and you have a wonderful memory in which you often relive past joys and sorrows. Deeply sentimental, you cling to your possessions with your crabby pincers, and probably have an attic

full of baby clothes, love letters and journals from your teenage years. Family heirlooms are especially treasured; even that ugly armchair your grandfather loved or the baby blanket with more holes than material embodies the love you felt for someone, or they for you. If you're honest, you don't really like throwing anything away. Some Cancer Moons hoard because subconsciously they feel protected by their stuff, and think if it vanished, they'd feel naked; you may even secretly believe that tatty old photographs have feelings that will be hurt if you throw them away.

Insecure

Being so emotionally attached to others, you naturally worry about losing their good opinion, and any little comments about the way you behave can be blown way out of proportion in that abundantly fertile imagination of yours. You don't always rise to the bait if you feel criticized, fearing that if you show others how easily you're knocked off balance, they'll think you're a bit unhinged. But even unintended criticism or an off-hand comment can quietly knock you sideways. You'll worry on your own about your perceived inadequacies and blame your losses in life on your appearance, shyness or insecurities instead of laughing at them for the thoughtless remarks they probably are. It's not as easy for you to dust yourself off and move on as it is for others, and you'll need a fair dose of reassurance to get back on your feet.

Sun and Moon combinations

Cancer Moon with **Aries Sun**

Independent, passionate and strong, you're a capable, fiery human. But underneath your opinionated, brave exterior is a deeply kind, loving and sentimental soul. You're choosy about who you allow to see your softer side in case they think you're a soft touch.

Cancer Moon with **Taurus Sun**

Comfort-loving and thoughtful, you like to take your time to make decisions and smell the roses. Stubborn and tenacious, when you set your heart on something you go after it quietly and patiently, but usually win your heart's desire. It can take a long time to get you to change your habits.

Cancer Moon with **Gemini Sun**

Intuitive and clever, you're aware of others' feelings, and surprise them with your psychic abilities. Constantly curious and a talented communicator,

you feel you can accomplish anything if you have a strong family base. Your wit disguises that you're actually easily hurt.

Cancer Moon with **Cancer Sun**

Your feelings change with the tides and the phases of the Moon; you're loving and open one minute, touchy and sensitive the next. You're tuned in to other people's feelings so much, it probably freaks them out a little. But your loyal, loving personality makes you a deeply kind and devoted friend or partner.

Cancer Moon with **Leo Sun**

You're dramatic, extravagant and emotional. You love being at the centre of a busy social scene, and you have strong family ties. Warm and vivacious, you love to organize games and days out. You hate to be ignored, but with your flamboyant character, that's not usually possible for long.

Cancer Moon with **Virgo Sun**

Warm, friendly and nurturing, you form lifelong friendships and are mindful of your loved ones' preferences and quirks. Impressively well-organized, you're trusted to look after the details and keep an eye on the purse strings. You're practical, with a huge heart.

Cancer Moon with **Libra Sun**

Indecisive but fair, you take a long time to reach a conclusion, but you'll always make the fairest decision possible. You're charming and social, and make friends easily. You are a true romantic; love and relationships have to be right in your life, even if everything else is chaotic.

Cancer Moon with **Scorpio Sun**

With a passionate depth of feeling, you probably understand the people you know better than they know themselves. You know everybody's secrets because you're so trustworthy, and you offer brilliant insights into your friends' and loved ones' problems. You're a fabulous friend and a terrifying enemy.

Cancer Moon with **Sagittarius Sun**

Cheerful and adventurous, you're an explorer who loves to push the boundaries and say yes to every experience — but you also love to return to your home comforts. You retreat into your shell and recuperate, then re-emerge fresh and ready to trek through the Peruvian jungle.

Cancer Moon with **Capricorn Sun**

Cautious but ambitious, you're an excellent businessperson with a big heart. You fool others with your quiet persistence and rarely shout about your successes. A traditionalist rather than a reformer, you have enormous respect for the past — and a photographic memory.

Cancer Moon with **Aquarius Sun**

Eccentric and brilliant, you're unpredictable, with a scientist's brain. You feel most relaxed when surrounded by family, friends and pets at home. Full of crazy ideas, you're friends with people from all walks of life — royalty and waifs and strays included.

Cancer Moon with **Pisces Sun**

One of the kindest and most sensitive people in the zodiac, you're a little shy, and prefer to go with the flow rather than draw attention to yourself. You have an incredible imagination and creative talents that need to be channelled — otherwise, you daydream or worry away your time.

MOON
IN
LEO

YOUR FIRST INSTINCTS

Stage-manage the situation

When your emotions rise to the surface, your proud inner Lion's gut reaction is to be the boss. Drifting along at the mercy of your unfettered feelings isn't your style, and whether you're dealing with anger, hurt or have fallen profoundly in love, you express your inner turmoil dramatically and with flair. Being caught emotionally unprepared keeps you awake at night. The only person to see you barefaced, hiding under a blanket, ugly-crying into a pillow is you. Acting swiftly to protect your pride, you'll channel your inner Scarlett O'Hara and brazenly, fabulously find a way to get what you want.

Create a narrative

Your theatrical Leo Moon compels you to process your emotions by finding a creative outlet that gives them meaning. Writing, listening to or playing music, cooking, crafting or any creative endeavour will help you work through periods when you feel confused, manic or disconnected. Leo is associated with the generative force of the Sun, so when it's your Moon sign, you discover yourself through exploring what you can bring to life. Whether you're organizing a wedding your friends will remember for years or selling macramé pot-plant holders online, your generous emotional instincts are to work through your feelings by giving. You feel alive when you bring your feelings, visions and ideas to life — in as vibrant and colourful a way as possible.

WHAT YOU'RE ATTRACTED TO IN OTHERS

Appreciation and encouragement

At heart you're a people-pleaser. You want to make people happy and bask in their attention when they need you. When you hear applause, or are complimented, you can't help but blossom in that good company. Some may accuse you of attention-seeking behaviour, but your need to be shown love, publicly and often, makes you work even harder to shower your loved ones with affection. You're drawn to people who respond to your positivity and exuberance, and when you receive a positive reaction or secure someone's attention, it fires you up. You want to shine, and when you see a spark of admiration in another's eyes, it fills you with joy — and you'll take that little bit of sparkle and create a whole universe of hope with it.

Unique qualities

You want glamour, style and drama from your relationships, so when you spot someone with a unique sense of style, you're intrigued. You like people who stand out from the crowd, and you like to be associated with popular, confident types who'll satisfy your thrill-seeking commitment to fun and pleasure. You also find it hard to resist slightly chaotic or disorganized types, because you know they'll appreciate you taking the lead sometimes. You're not just a pretty face, and your Leo Moon needs to be admired for your brain, excellent taste and capable personality too. The more special others make you feel, the more precious they are to you.

YOUR FEARS AND EMOTIONAL RESPONSES

Love me, hate me, but don't ignore me

Your fear of being ignored is probably the last problem people who know you would imagine you have. To others, you're confident, brave and even a little over the top. But under all the flamboyance, smoke and mirrors, your self-esteem is tied up with other people's opinions of you. When that opinion is good, you glow. But if someone you care about hasn't called you for a while, or their attention is elsewhere, you wilt like spinach in boiling water. Under your ebullient exterior, you harbour a very tender heart and can feel deeply wounded if someone else catches your partner's eye or a friend blocks you on social media.

Anything but ordinary

No Leo Moon person should be made to feel ordinary. You were put on this earth to shine, so when — as happens with everyone now and then — you lose your mojo, underperform, or can't summon enough energy to keep your socks up, you worry that you're actually no more spectacular than anyone else. But, of course, this is not true — you're just much harsher on yourself about it than anyone else would be. To you, ordinary means uninteresting, unworthy and pointless, but sometimes not standing out can be liberating. You don't have to live up to high expectations, you can slip by unrecognized in the supermarket, shopping in your PJs, and you don't have to think of something witty to say to the colleague who spotted you at your part-time window-cleaning job.

WHAT YOU KEEP SECRET

Jealousy stings

If someone else has the attention you crave, you bleed. After all, you're the person who works hardest to be in the limelight… so when someone appears to steal it from you, it can feel personal. Naturally, you'd never admit to something as debasing as jealousy. Even though there isn't a human on earth who's not experienced jealousy, you'll rarely admit to being like other humans. Unfortunately, this means when it catches you off guard, it floors you. Under your jealousy there's admiration, which is a reliable indicator of your true desires. Trying to ignore or suppress envy means it pops up in ugly ways, but accepting the uncomfortable feelings can offer you useful pointers to what will make you truly happy.

You shine, but you're not reflective

Not one to dwell on past mistakes or think too deeply about your motivation, you can come across as a little shallow or self-centred at times. But what you don't tell others is that you just don't spend much time going over the past or feeling regretful. What's done is done, and you don't go in for self-shaming. You may appear to chide yourself, for appearances' sake, but you save your remorse and try to look forward to more cheerful things. Life's too short to not burn brightly one hundred percent of the time. And besides, you forgive and forget others' mistakes and expect them to do the same.

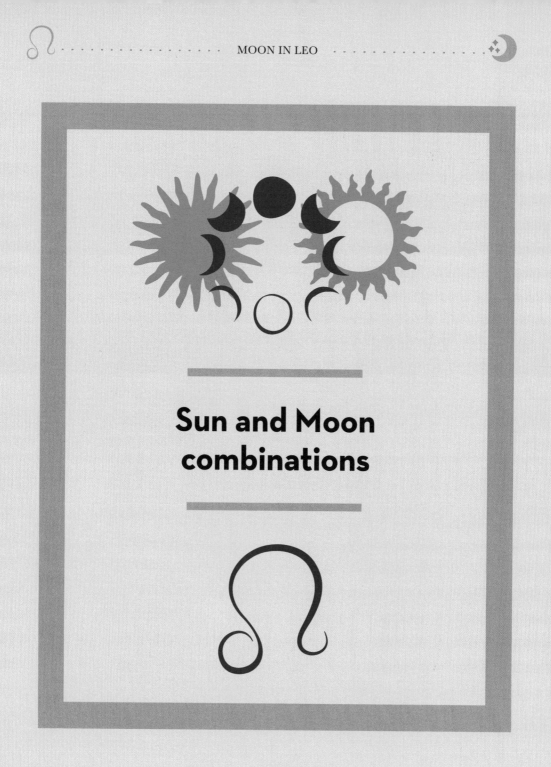

Sun and Moon combinations

♌

Leo Moon with **Aries Sun**

You enjoy a challenge, and on the surface you're a strong, independent character. Underneath your confident personality, you seek approval and want to make an unforgettable impression on the world. Spontaneous and fun, you easily attract friends and lovers. You're intensely hurt when things don't work out, but you also move on swiftly when things come to an end.

Leo Moon with **Taurus Sun**

Strong, confident and a little stubborn, you power through life's challenges with grace and flair. When you make decisions, you see them out, and you're a trustworthy partner and friend. You've an eye for a bargain, but your love of luxury means your money's spent as soon as it arrives. But somehow you still seem to live in the lap of luxury.

Leo Moon with **Gemini Sun**

A cheerful, bubbly person, you keep centred with family life. But you're a happy traveller, too, with an inquisitive, friendly way with strangers. Outgoing and comfortable in the spotlight, you may enjoy dance, theatre and organizing parties. You're generous with your time, and your social life is rich with friends from all walks of life.

Leo Moon with **Cancer Sun**

You're never more comfortable than when you're surrounded by your family in your castle, your home. You're a wonderful organizer, and you can be bossy, but you see it as helping your loved ones reach their potential. Emotionally intelligent, you're kind-hearted and moody, and skilled at looking after the people you care for.

Leo Moon with **Leo Sun**

You're giving and headstrong, a leader who's not afraid to take charge. Dominant and direct, you face challenges head-on and are enormously kind to the people you love — but you're a mortal enemy if you take a dislike to someone. A little vain, you're approval-seeking and easily flattered.

Leo Moon with **Virgo Sun**

You're a big planner, ambitious and good with details because you can envision the whole picture. You can be critical or pushy sometimes, but your perfectionist tendencies mean you can easily spot flaws that can be improved. Witty and entertaining, you make the dullest subjects sound fun, and are an inspiring teacher.

Leo Moon with **Libra Sun**

Popular and charming, you know how to get through to people, and you're an excellent judge of character. Always fair and compassionate, you sometimes give your power away to avoid conflict. You're diplomatic and relationship-focused, a romantic soul with the imaginative power to turn your dreams into reality.

Leo Moon with **Scorpio Sun**

Mysterious and dynamic, you have a ruthless, sexy reputation and you like to keep it that way. People who know you well know that you're kind-hearted and warm, but you prefer to stay a little emotionally distant from people you don't know that well, as it takes you a while to trust new people.

Leo Moon with **Sagittarius Sun**

A force of nature, when you get an exciting idea into your head you're restless, impatient and excitable. You're organized with vision, but when it comes to practical details you can be sketchy. Flamboyant and endlessly enthusiastic, you brighten any company with your cheery optimism.

Leo Moon with **Capricorn Sun**

There's no stopping you when you have your sights set on something or someone you want. You're methodical and energetic, and have oodles of self-belief. You're quietly confident, and others often underestimate your impressive creative skills. But when you get an opportunity to shine, you grab it like a life jacket.

Leo Moon with **Aquarius Sun**

You've an ever-growing circle of friends and acquaintances and are drawn to support humanitarian causes. You love leading and working with groups and teams — the more people the better. You shine when asked for your opinion or creative input, and pleasantly surprise everyone with your eccentric but genius ideas.

Leo Moon with **Pisces Sun**

You are an imaginative visionary, and your intuition is hot. You might not be the most practical person on the planet, but you're the most creative. You always see the best in people and inspire everyone with your compassionate, gentle nature. You turn sceptics into believers and villains into heroes.

YOUR FIRST INSTINCTS

Organize the heck out of things

If you're facing a big day, feeling unsure of yourself, or need to calm the hell down, your initial gut feeling is to tidy up — you can't think if there are dirty dishes lying around or dog hair on the couch because it disturbs your emotional tranquillity. Keep the organizing to a specific amount of time; otherwise you'll end up defrosting the freezer when, actually, you need to write a report by lunchtime. Your conscientious Virgo Moon means you rarely turn down work and can even find it hard to relax if you don't have a deadline on the horizon. If you have a clear desk, a pleasant environment and some delightful stationery, you're invincible — ready to take on whatever the world chooses to chuck at you.

Analyze, refine and perfect

Your mind and body are rarely still, and it's the same for you on an emotional level. You're in a constant state of betterment, refining and editing your thoughts and feelings, correcting your mistakes and learning from them. Your hyper-nervous system is in persistent flux, always working to be a perfect human. You find details soothing — digesting and adjusting the small stuff so the machine runs efficiently. Good nutrition, a professional work ethic, being kind to your loved ones and organizing the world around you bring you solace. Unfairly, you may have a reputation for being a harsh critic, but that's not your intention. Your emotional style is to understand your emotions, and to spot flaws and untangle them. You welcome others' advice, and are hurt when loved ones take your well-meant observations the wrong way.

WHAT YOU'RE ATTRACTED TO IN OTHERS

Healing qualities

Doctors, physios, aromatherapists and counsellors have your approval. You need healing, calming people in your life and are attracted to their soothing qualities. Your perfectionism can sometimes leak into hypochondria or obsessive tendencies to check and recheck that you've completed certain tasks properly. You can worry yourself into a stomach ache or may discover you can't make love to your partner until the recycling's been taken out. You need someone who can help you relax — or at least who doesn't make you more anxious. Someone chilled will help with your insomnia, as will a partner who knows how to meditate. An interest in health and medicine will make you feel more secure, and stop you worrying that you have necrotizing fasciitis every time you get an itchy nose.

Quiet revolutionaries

You're subtle and modest, and high drama and emotional outbursts alarm you. Clever, quiet types make your heart beat a little faster with their witty, self-depreciating style. Emotionally, you find the strong, silent type very alluring, and if they're also working studiously on a plan to make the world a simpler and more efficient place — you're hooked. Practicality over idealism wins your heart; you love people who actually do what they say rather than just talk about it. Because you're usually the one implementing the bulk of the work in your partnerships, you also find it sexy when you meet someone with sharp life skills. A decent cook, a sensible head for money and someone who cleans up after themselves will flip your lid and melt your heart.

YOUR FEARS AND EMOTIONAL RESPONSES

Chaos and spontaneity

You're a planner. You protect your kind, shy emotional core by paying great attention to exactly what's happening around you. You like time to understand how you feel about things, and if you're put on the spot it makes you uncomfortable. Your idea of hell is to start at a new company where you're suddenly the centre of attention — and asked to share a little-known fact about yourself. If warned, you'd have an amusing, apparently spontaneous anecdote to share with your audience. Instead, you're just staring at a bit of fluff on your jacket hoping it will beam you off to another dimension. You're good at giving things your full attention and focus, but when you're the one under the microscope, you squirm.

Quit making sense of the illogical

To lessen the pain of uncomfortable feelings, you give yourself sensible-sounding advice. You know you *ought* not to feel jealous of your successful but humble brain-surgeon cousin with the fabulous hair — but you are. It stings that you still feel hurt by your ex's swift marriage after you split up — but you still send them funny cat memes. Sometimes you don't know what's good for you, and you can be harder on yourself than anyone else. Ditch the shaky friendships that make you feel bad. Knowing you shouldn't feel sad, envious or hurt doesn't make it less real. Admit you're human; you, more than any other Moon sign, need to cut yourself some slack. Awkward feelings are just part of life.

WHAT YOU KEEP SECRET

You make mistakes

You feel your blunders in an intensely personal way, but you learn hard from your mistakes. You're naturally modest, and certainly not a fan of drawing attention to yourself. You won't advertise that it took you 10 years to realize that co-workers weren't farming colleagues, or that you need glasses as thick as Scooby snacks to find your phone in the morning. It's true that your friends and loved ones rely on your excellent judgment and impeccable taste — add that to you being so damn right about everything. But they'd probably find it endearing that you think Guantánamo is a musical, not a place, and that you still have your My Little Pony collection. Sharing your failings or perceived weaknesses brings empathy and understanding when you're feeling vulnerable, and makes your bloopers feel less threatening.

Surprisingly sexy

Your cool, unassuming personality helps you filter out people you find distasteful or alarming, and the ones who make it through your refining, critical scrutiny are in for a surprise. When you trust someone and let them into your private world, you blossom. You give your heart easily to the right person, and when you relax, you're passionate and sensual. Self-acceptance is harder for you than most, so when you find someone who convinces you of their love, it can be a freeing experience. You long to merge with another and forget yourself for a while, and for you love is a healing experience on a profound level.

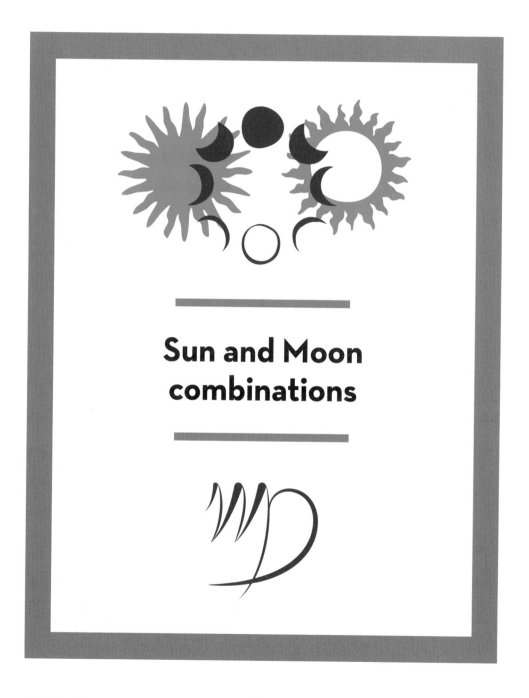

Sun and Moon combinations

Virgo Moon with **Aries Sun**

A superhuman planner, you're direct but humble, and brilliant at getting to the heart of what really matters. You're quick to make decisions and give good advice, whether your friends want to hear it or not. You're a tough cookie, but when you let your defences down you're a true romantic.

Virgo Moon with **Taurus Sun**

Always practical, you consider life's challenges from all angles before making decisions, and your friends and family trust your wise opinions. You love your home comforts, have good knowledge of food and nutrition, and appreciate quality furnishings. You also need an organized, tidy environment to help you unwind.

Virgo Moon with **Gemini Sun**

You're fuelled by information and feel your most secure when you have healthy, free-flowing communication with the people around you. It's vital that you feel safe sharing your thoughts and feelings with your closest companions, and you feel at your best when you're the one doing the organizing, as you don't trust others will do a better job!

Virgo Moon with **Cancer Sun**

An insightful combination of emotionally intelligent and sensitive, you worry about your loved ones and protect them ferociously. You are shy but tenacious; others may underestimate you at times, but you work steadily toward your goals and shine in your career. Your natural modesty keeps you from crowing and endears you to your loved ones.

Virgo Moon with **Leo Sun**

Audacious and popular, you're not always as confident as you make out, but you never let that shine through.

Your creative Leo Sun wants to bring new ideas to life, and your hardworking, detail-oriented Virgo Moon instils you with determination and stamina to make it happen. You're a good leader, organized, thorough and kind.

Virgo Moon with **Virgo Sun**

Perfectionist and industrious, you can be hard on yourself, but you're kind and thoughtful of your loved ones and offer excellent health and wellbeing advice. You always look for neat, logical solutions to challenges, and you keep your emotions in check. But your feelings are more easily hurt than the people around you realize.

Virgo Moon with **Libra Sun**

You are romantic and partnership-focused. Your relationships are a priority, but you can be very choosy about who you end up with. It can take you an age to make up your mind about the important things in life — partly because you like to go into intense detail and partly because you want to make a fair decision.

Virgo Moon with **Scorpio Sun**

Something of a dark horse, you can be quiet and unassuming when people don't know you well, but when your emotions are touched you're passionate, mysterious and cool. Good with money, you're tight with the purse strings but will go all out for quality and craftsmanship.

Virgo Moon with **Sagittarius Sun**

Vivacious and broad-minded, you attract fun, outgoing types into your orbit. You're a little reluctant to commit to long-term relationships, but you have a truckload of adoring pals. You may appear to be happy-go-lucky on the outside, but that's only after careful consideration and analysis on the inside.

Virgo Moon with **Capricorn Sun**

Thoughtful, methodical and a little cynical, you're an enterprising person with discipline running through your veins. You're always working and planning your next fabulous move, but you probably should take time to chill out and go on dates. Don't leave your love life to wither.

Virgo Moon with **Aquarius Sun**

Free-spirited, aloof and original, you make up your own rules. You're usually five steps ahead of everyone else, but it's important that you let the rest of the world catch up with you; otherwise you can feel a little disconnected. You can be emotionally inscrutable, and back away when you feel others becoming too close.

Virgo Moon with **Pisces Sun**

There's a mesmerizing balance between your imaginative, ethereal and slightly chaotic Pisces Sun and your strait-laced, health-conscious Virgo Moon. You're always trying to find a sensible level between your good and bad habits, and you have a charismatic aura that draws people to you.

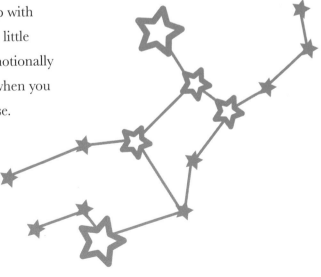

MOON
IN
LIBRA

YOUR FIRST INSTINCTS

Fierce peacekeeper

Your emotional landscape needs to be harmonious, and if something knocks you off balance it makes you anxious. Whether you're trying to get to grips with your anger, uncertainty or excitement, your initial impulse is to keep things level, cordial and pleasant. If you're facing an emotional challenge or crisis, you take the metaphorical temperature of the people around you, to make sure they're all on good terms with you and each other. You have an antenna attuned to others' welfare, and you'll know when something is amiss. And because your own feelings are dependent on the wellbeing of the people you care about, their happiness sometimes matters more than it ought to.

Be likeable

The scales of justice are your zodiac symbol, and you're so sensitive to the atmosphere tipping out of balance that you can see conflict arising before anyone else has a whiff that something might be amiss. Your charm is your superpower and, in your experience, nobody wins any prizes or gets what they want by being provocative or aggressive. You gain emotional sustenance from knowing that your relationships are healthy, and take great comfort that your loved ones are there when you need them. Conflict is unavoidable at times, and goes against your diplomatic instincts. But if you have to tell someone something they don't want to hear, you'll do it in the kindest, least destructive way possible. Even after breakups, divorces or friendship-busting disagreements, you do your best to stay friends.

WHAT YOU'RE ATTRACTED TO IN OTHERS

Your other half

Libra is the zodiac sign most associated with partnership, love and romance. You were born looking for close relationships, and you long to find your other half, the person who brings harmony and balances your scales. You're a clever person who likes to keep your mind busy, and you enjoy being out socializing at a new restaurant and checking out the latest arty films. You hope to meet someone who shares your appreciation of style and culture and likes to take care of their appearance. You've been known to change your outfit three times before going to the supermarket, so you'll welcome someone with a similar attitude to looking good. Craftsmanship, quality and taste are important to you, but you also love it when others are confident enough to snap you out of your perfectionism and fussing, and help you see the joy in what's right in front of you.

Decisive charmers

Because you place so much of your energy into being nice to people, and usually give in to their demands, you find people who are the opposite hard to resist. You secretly admire confident types who say exactly what they think or express exactly what they feel without caring too much about how anyone else will react. You'll avoid confrontation at all costs because you don't want to upset anyone, even if they are in the wrong. The thought of an assertive, persuasive partner is appealing, and a companion who defends and sticks up for what you want is super-enticing. If left to your own devices, you could agonize over every tiny decision, so you might enjoy a person who can help you discriminate and make quicker choices.

YOUR FEARS AND EMOTIONAL RESPONSES

Being alone

At the heart of your obsession with fairness, symmetry and looking as good as possible is a fear that if you're not perfect, you'll not find a partner. As you're such a relationship-obsessed person, being on your own is not where you want to end up. Making sure you're always in others' good books can drain your energy

and make you feel insecure, and your neediness can drive people away. Trying too hard and courting approval from a potential partner, friend or colleague could make them feel under pressure to respond to you kindly, rather than just letting the relationship happen naturally on their own terms. Give people some breathing space and don't worry so much. You're a lovely person, so just relax and let things progress spontaneously.

Wrong decisions

You're in a process of constant analysis and balance, making sure your decisions and judgments are the best they can be. But constantly worrying about even the smallest choices can drive you a little crazy. Overthinking can cause you sleepless nights over things that don't matter in the morning, and trivial details can get blown way out of proportion. Let yourself be wrong about something inconsequential and you'll see the world does not stop turning. You're especially prone to going back over your thinking process after a disagreement with someone you care about. In some way, you are trying to protect and defend yourself against being mistaken, constantly adjusting your feelings and thinking to be balanced and fair.

WHAT YOU KEEP SECRET

You always cave in

Although your Libra Moon sign is the most obsessed with love and relationships, your emotions can be elusive. It's hard for you to voice your anger or stand your ground when someone is being difficult, which can give people the wrong impression: that you're passive or just agree with the person you interacted with. The truth is, you cannot bear the idea of hurting or offending anyone, and you crumble to avoid others' anger or even mild annoyance. You might accept the blame for something you didn't do or pay way over the odds for a haircut you hate, all in the name of avoiding confrontation.

Your own truth

Prioritizing others' feelings and opinions means sacrificing some of your own truth, but secretly you reckon that if the people you love are happy, then you will be too. Even if you agree that you should be tougher or more direct with people you think may be taking advantage of your good nature, asserting yourself can make you feel vulnerable and massively out of your comfort zone. You cultivate tranquil, loving relationships, and your partner, friends or family could be upset if they knew that you just pretend to like rock climbing, watching football, or building model railways just because they do. Magical stuff happens when you stand up for yourself, and your relationships will improve — which is always your goal.

Sun and Moon combinations

Libra Moon with **Aries Sun**

Your Aries Sun offers you independence and a decisive sense of direction, but your Libra moon keeps you scrupulously fair. Romantic and passionate, you put a great deal of energy into your relationships, and your love life is rarely dull. You're honest, and a straight-talker, and you're hurt when others aren't.

Libra Moon with **Taurus Sun**

A lover of beauty, you're drawn to art, music and crafts, and you love beautiful clothes and luxurious surroundings. You don't mind spending money on quality, but you have a big appetite for fashion, food and socializing. Your steady, fair nature attracts a wide circle of friends who become as important as your family.

Libra Moon with **Gemini Sun**

Flirty and talkative, you gracefully multitask and can hold three conversations at once. Always weighing up the pros and cons, you gather information quickly from your ever-tingling antennae. If you don't know something, it's probably not worth knowing. You find it easy to get along with people from all walks of life.

Libra Moon with **Cancer Sun**

Keeping good relationships with your family is vital for you; if everything is going well with them, you feel at peace. You fight for the people you care about and tirelessly defend them. Your Libra moon means you're sensitive to any tension with loved ones, and you won't rest until peace is restored.

Libra Moon with **Leo Sun**

Popular and glamorous, you understand how to entertain people while being in tune with their emotional needs. You're well-organized and a natural leader, though you have a soft, romantic side that dislikes conflict. You have an eye for beautiful clothes and objects, and impulsive spending habits that could need taming.

Libra Moon with **Virgo Sun**

Studious and wise, you consider problems from all angles before making a move. You're skilled at handling tense situations, and the people close to you rely on your calming, sensible influence. You can be critical of your imagined imperfections, and it can take you a while to realize that nobody else is judging you.

Libra Moon with **Libra Sun**

Charming and social, you know how to work a room, and have a sixth sense when it comes to planning the perfect gathering. You have a designer's good taste and do everything in your power to avoid arguments or ugly scenes. Loved ones respect your opinion, even if it does take years for you to decide.

Libra Moon with **Scorpio Sun**

You have a mysterious air that hints at sexy depths. Saving your energy for when it's most needed, you're quiet and still on the outside, but emotionally you're always deciding on the best course of action. You're an intriguing synthesis of balance and an all-or-nothing approach, so when you know what you want, you pursue it fiercely.

Libra Moon with **Sagittarius Sun**

You're a live-for-the-moment person, delighted by life's possibilities, but it's difficult for you to plan or save money. Vigorously knowledgeable and never short of opinions, on the outside you're confident and energetic. Emotionally, you're less sure of yourself, but your willingness to please others just adds to your exuberant charm.

Libra Moon with **Capricorn Sun**

You have excellent judgment and rarely rush into anything without careful forethought and planning. You have a traditional approach to work and family life, and are happy to shoulder tough responsibilities. Witty and charming, you know how to put people at ease. But beneath your polished professionalism, you're a romantic at heart.

Libra Moon with **Aquarius Sun**

Great at making friends, you're quirky and funny, and you shine when you're in a team or group of like-minded people. Your original ideas and quick intelligence help you form lifelong bonds. You're not one for being on your own; the more people around you, the better.

Libra Moon with **Pisces Sun**

Imaginative and compassionate, you have amazing insight into others' behaviour. You're a soft-hearted, generous person who believes everyone deserves a chance, and you place trust in anyone who does you a good turn. Romantic to your core, you believe that love conquers all, even if you've been hurt in the past.

MOON
IN
SCORPIO

YOUR FIRST INSTINCTS

Get in deep

You're an intensely emotional person and are generally better at hiding strong emotions than other zodiac signs. Your instinctive response to challenges is to look at the underlying motivation for your tumultuous emotions. You want the truth — and you can take it. You're more forgiving of your darker feelings than most, and you don't shy away from the fact that jealousy, greed and revenge are part of being human. Understanding the lengths others go to to keep their uncomfortable feelings private actually makes you a wonderful person to confide in. You can see past other people's emotional smokescreens to the heart of what is really driving them, and you feel others' pain when you know they're doing their best to disguise it.

Keep schtum

Unusually perceptive about the true nature of your own feelings, you like to keep things to yourself. Your Scorpio Moon helps you pull your emotions from the darkest, most hidden places inside yourself. But you bravely examine them in the light of your own consciousness, where you can transform your feelings and start the healing process. In your heart you know that to be free of emotional pain, you have to get back to the source and fully relive the humiliation, hurt or loss. Only then can you be reborn. This has to be a private process, because beneath your scary Scorpion image, you're all exposed nerves, with a heart as thin as an eggshell. The thought of anyone discovering that you're as sensitive as a porcupine in a balloon factory terrifies you.

WHAT YOU'RE ATTRACTED TO IN OTHERS

Loyalty and serenity

Although Scorpio has a ruthless, sexy image to uphold, what you actually need in a relationship is security. You enjoy unruffled, patient people because you are fascinated by their composure — something you may feel you lack emotionally. You're subtle when you find someone attractive, and your feelings will be intense — but you'll not want to show your hand for a while. You play the long game when it comes to love, and you're not interested in a shallow affair. You don't make it easy for others to get to know you; to catch your eye, your potential

partner should respond carefully, be discreet and take you seriously. You need to be sure you're not flirting with someone who broadcasts your every move on social media before you let down your drawbridge.

Beyond sexy

You swoon at the thought of a slow-burning, uniting-of-souls sexual experience, where you merge with each other in spiritual ecstasy. So a 'chuck me over your shoulder caveman style' approach isn't going to work for you. A willingness to experiment will turn you on, but you're a strictly monogamous type, and desire the same commitment from your other half. You don't just want hairy, sweaty, messy sex — you're on a quest to attain a higher level of consciousness with the person you love, and you need to be sure that you're both on the same level. You see sex as the ultimate emotional experience, and need someone who will welcome, rather than run from, your intensity.

YOUR FEARS AND EMOTIONAL RESPONSES

Betrayal

As someone who gives all in love and friendship, you're hurt to your core when someone you welcomed into your inner sanctum rejects you. Part of the reason you're so cagey about sharing your feelings is that you want to be in control. Shocks on this level feel intolerable because there's nothing you can do about it. It could be that you experienced a gut-wrenching heartbreak when you were younger and decided there and then that nobody was going to hurt you in the same way, ever again. When you're offended or hurt now, you're dumbfounded, and nobody wants to be on the wrong side of a hurt Scorpio. Revenge will only seem fair. Your favourite form of retribution comes after you have quietly but completely processed the pain — then you're quite capable of cleanly and remorselessly cutting people from your life.

Deadly stinger

Everyone knows what happens if a scorpion gets defensive — it protects itself by injecting its enemy with venom. Ordinarily you're not a vengeful type, but if your worst fears are realized, or you feel taken advantage of, you can be a devastating enemy. Perhaps you trusted and confided in someone and they used what you said against you. What people don't realize about you is that you're brilliant at unearthing other people's secrets and discovering their weak spots. You never forget, just in case you need them as ammunition at a later date. A little like owning a nuclear deterrent — you never share your secrets without some in exchange. When you trust someone, they'll know where you hurt, and you'll know where they hurt. If one of you pushes the other's button, you'll destroy each other.

WHAT YOU KEEP SECRET

Everything

When you gain someone's trust, you take it as a great honour. If a friend wishes to share that they're a secret billionaire, or they think your dad is hot, you'll take this knowledge to the grave. People open up to people who can keep secrets, and sometimes you'll wish they wouldn't. It might help your friend to unburden that they're having an affair, but if you know their partner you're going to wish they hadn't told you. This is partly why Scorpio Moon people get to see the darker side of life — you get told the truth and are trusted to keep it. Knowledge is power, even if you don't intend on using it. But it can give you confidence that you have something to fight back with if you were ever in a life-or-death situation.

Does everyone feel like this?

Because you're always trying to keep the lid on your own intense emotions, you assume everyone is the same — fronting things out, pretending not to care. Can it be possible that others appear calm and collected because underneath their mask, they actually are? Sometimes when your emotions threaten to overwhelm you, you wonder if it's just you who is constantly knocked sideways by anger, remorse, lust or excitement. You'd love to talk to your loved ones about it, but that means sharing your vulnerability — what if they think you're an emotional wreck? You are pretty attached to your inner drama, and you study your loved ones' highs and lows to see if they are too.

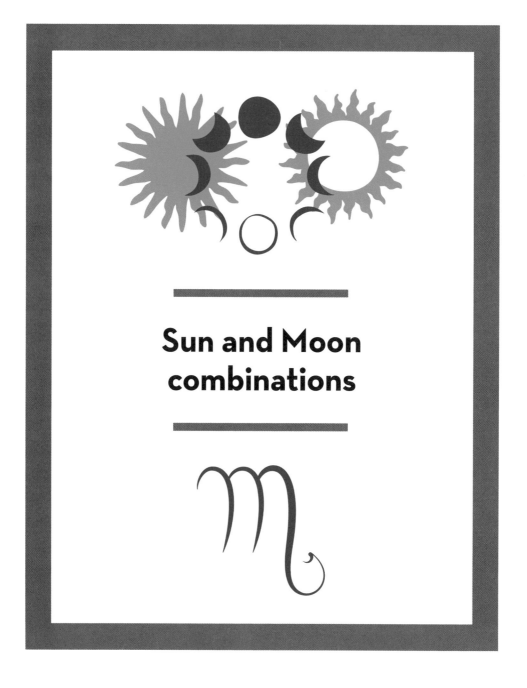

Sun and Moon combinations

Scorpio Moon with **Aries Sun**

Mysterious but warm and spontaneous, you have a quick temper, but you don't hold grudges for long. Your fiery confidence and impressive willpower mean you're a natural leader, though you're guarded about your private life. Others would be surprised if they knew what a romantic soul lurks beneath your tough exterior.

Scorpio Moon with **Taurus Sun**

You like to conserve your energy for when you really need it, which gives you a calm aura. You're a steady, self-assured type on the outside, but emotionally you're dynamic, restless and passionate. You rarely give up on projects or people and tend to get even more obsessed with your interests as you get older.

Scorpio Moon with **Gemini Sun**

Clever and emotionally intelligent, you're skilled at understanding the people around you on a profound level. Your instincts are white-hot, and you can tell when someone isn't being honest with you. You love a mystery and can tunnel to the truth of any situation just by asking a few pertinent questions.

Scorpio Moon with **Cancer Sun**

Deeply kind and empathic, you're one of the most sensitive people in the zodiac. Keeping yourself to yourself, you're shy and unassuming, but when you love someone you protect them with fervent zeal and adoration. You're wonderful at looking after people and are a loyal, loving friend and partner.

Scorpio Moon with **Leo Sun**

Energetic and charismatic, you're strong-willed and focused when achieving your goals. Outwardly generous and warm, inside you battle strong, dramatic emotions. You're an enigma wrapped in a mystery, glamorous and popular, with creative flair and impeccable taste, and you never back down from a promise.

Scorpio Moon with **Virgo Sun**

You're so organized, you arrange your week-ahead outfits on Sunday evening and even iron your socks. You like to be prepared for any possibility. You dislike surprises, as spontaneity could reveal your real feelings, and you'd take a long walk in the country over attending a work social event any time.

Scorpio Moon with **Libra Sun**

Seductive and hypnotic, you're sexy without trying and you draw people into your orbit. You're people-pleasing on the outside, but your good manners and political correctness mask a wilder, less graceful emotional

side. A little obsessed with love, most of your worries are concentrated on your other half, or lack of one.

Scorpio Moon with **Scorpio Sun**

You have the kind of smouldering depth that drives people to get to know you better. You keep yourself to yourself, and you hint at tortured depths, which either compels people into your orbit or drives them away. A faithful friend, you stick to your loved ones like glue.

Scorpio Moon with **Sagittarius Sun**

Self-sufficient and intense, there's little that stands in your way when you set your sights on something. You are intellectually curious, with a passionate centre; life rarely feels dull when you're around. You inspire your friends and colleagues with your tireless enthusiasm and energy to power through problems.

Scorpio Moon with **Capricorn Sun**

Responsible and steady, you take care of the people around you and put their needs first. It can take you a long time to trust people, but once you do, you share everything. Determined to succeed, you love a practical plan and measured results. Slow but thorough, you always reach your goals.

Scorpio Moon with **Aquarius Sun**

Your light and breezy outer personality is a contrast to your intense emotional side. You have a unique take on life and tend to be the odd one out in a gathering. You laugh in the face of rules and tradition, but when it comes to love you're deep, loyal and passionate.

Scorpio Moon with **Pisces Sun**

Thoughtful and sensitive, you can sense a tense atmosphere before you've stepped inside a room. You're shy but determined and loving, and keep a tight hold on the people you care about. Emotionally dynamic, you've learned to wait awhile before declaring your true feelings, as how you feel varies from minute to minute.

MOON
IN
SAGITTARIUS

YOUR FIRST INSTINCTS

The spirit of adventure

You are gregarious, cheerful and frank. Your gut reaction to new challenges is to see them as an opportunity for personal growth and adventure. You want to learn as much as possible from your experience and are hopeful that, even if you're taken aback, apprehensive or sad, you'll get a chance to find answers to some of life's philosophical questions. You tackle emotionally challenging situations with an admirable, carefree confidence and a smile on your face. If your plans don't work out, you bounce fearlessly, and sometimes recklessly, into the next exciting thing that takes your fancy. Never one to be accused of self-pity or excessive brooding, you're determined to laugh in the face of anything the rest of the world wants you to take seriously.

Faith and optimism

Your faith in human goodness is inspiring and comes from your knowledge that life has endless possibilities. Your constant quest for the truth keeps you feeling alive, and your restless, emotional nature leaps from one extrovert enthusiasm to the next. There's no time for sadness or reflection in your world, but because of your all-or-nothing personality, you do occasionally suffer from emotional extremes — usually excitement and nervousness rather than anything too introverted or consuming. You're generous with your warmth and enthusiasm, and your bad-taste jokes at inappropriate times will always hit the right note if friends and family are feeling down. Your motto is, 'Everything will be all right in the end, and if it's not all right, it's not the end.'

WHAT YOU'RE ATTRACTED TO IN OTHERS

Intellectual challenge

You want to share your knowledge with people who will be as excited to join your quest for experience, travel and knowledge as you are. Not one to sit at home watching what's going on in the world on TV, you want to be out there in the thick of it, and you wish for a partner who feels the same. Suspicious of emotionally quiet characters, you don't trust people who are shy about proclaiming their feelings and don't appear to get upset. You are thick-skinned and probably think people who are hard to read are hiding their truth. You gravitate to people who are loud, proud and confident about their thoughts and feelings. Excited by challenges, you're drawn to the buzzy energy of competitive types. Chatty, funny, outgoing people who stick up for their beliefs will leave a lasting impression.

Focus and nuance

You're a little commitment-phobic and emotionally restless; whoever wins your full attention will have rare qualities. Emotionally, you're a bigger-picture type of person who gets bored with practicalities and details, and you admire people who choose a life free of traditional ties and responsibilities. But you need a partner who can make you stop, think and look deeper. In your enthusiastic, rough-and-ready bluster, you could be missing fascinating details about the people around you. One of your life's greatest lessons is learning when to stay rooted to absorb more experiences, and when to gallop off to the next challenge. A partner who teaches you a more nuanced, emotionally forensic approach will open a richly rewarding world for you to explore together.

YOUR FEARS AND EMOTIONAL RESPONSES

Restraint and restriction

You don't like being told what to do — not by your parents, your boss or the government. You'll choose the path you follow, and anyone who wants you to toe the line will meet with a blunt response. You thrive in an environment where you can be spontaneous and pursue your opinions, theories or beliefs freely. You make your own rules and live by a unique set of standards, so when you're asked to stick to anyone else's petty regulations, you feel stifled and rebellious. You wear your heart on your sleeve and can be emotionally extreme, so anyone you're unhappy with will have no doubts about how you feel.

Boredom

Emotionally, you want to feel that you're learning and growing every day. You're a fantastically curious person, and when something piques your interest, you get sucked down all sorts of rabbit holes searching for knowledge and truth, whether that's exploring Byzantine mosaics and frescoes or the religious beliefs of the African Dogon tribe. Initially, you're passionate about your discovery and throw yourself into your new interest with the subtlety of a shark attack. But you lose interest after you hungrily digest all the juicy bits. Well-known for juggling several projects at once, and in all directions, you feel uncomfortable finishing what you start because for you to feel alive, you must keep your curiosity and quest for knowledge going.

WHAT YOU KEEP SECRET

You don't know when to stop

You do everything in a big way, and your Sagittarius Moon expresses your love of life with a generous spirit and emotional eagerness. When you enjoy something, you want more, and you never want it to stop. Hating to be restrained by boring necessities like money or political correctness, you indulge and emotionally expand to fit your passions. You've a Bacchanalian appetite for food and fun, a librarian's lust for books, and a poker player's compulsion for gambling. But all that spending, hoarding and consuming can take you to some dark places that challenge your indomitable lust for life. You keep your excesses private, but they can eat away at you if you ignore them altogether.

Run from your problems

When life gets too much, or you feel emotionally overwhelmed, there's a strong temptation to run as fast as your hairy, half-man, half-horse Sagittarius Moon legs will carry you. You may have broken someone's heart when you realized you didn't want to settle down, or maybe you got into a financial pickle and disappeared before there was time to explain yourself to anyone involved. You're anything but cold-hearted, and will have done your best with whatever situation you were dealing with at the time, but you're probably no stranger to pining for fresh pastures and longing to start a new life somewhere else. There are probably a couple of skeletons in your cupboard, and that's where you intend to keep them.

Sun and Moon combinations

Sagittarius Moon with **Aries Sun**

A forthright and at times outspoken person, you live for the moment and don't look back. Forever the optimist, you inspire everyone around you with your energy. You feel life to the full, and everyone close to you knows exactly how you feel because you're open, honest and frank with your opinions.

Sagittarius Moon with **Taurus Sun**

Nature-loving and adventurous, you love being outside, gardening and hiking with the occasional stay in a luxurious hotel. A loyal friend and partner, your relationships are warm and stable, but emotionally you have a wild streak that cries out for freedom and new experiences.

Sagittarius Moon with **Gemini Sun**

When you're interested in something or someone, you soak up every detail and become a master of your subject. You're fantastically good at obsessing and cramming in facts, but you're fickle and lose interest as quickly as you began. Warm and funny, you're popular, intelligent and can't sit still for five minutes.

Sagittarius Moon with **Cancer Sun**

Generous and expressive, you have big emotions and feel most at home at the heart of a busy household. Family means the world to you, but your restless Sagittarius Moon means you're also fascinated by different cultures and want to explore all the world has to offer.

Sagittarius Moon with **Leo Sun**

Your social life is the stuff of legend, as you're generous, outgoing and a little extravagant. You're happy in the spotlight and can feel a bit lonely when you're not centre stage. Spontaneous and freedom-loving, you're most people's choice when they need cheering up.

Sagittarius Moon with **Virgo Sun**

A bundle of outgoing and modest character traits, you're quiet and thoughtful with people you don't know, but once you're friends it's hard to shut you up. You veer from worrying about the state of the world to throwing caution to the wind, and it seems to suit you.

Sagittarius Moon with **Libra Sun**

Social, glamorous and outspoken, you're never short of friends. It's hard for you to make decisions because you're so honest and fair-minded. You can see both sides of most arguments, but your diplomacy skills mean you can make even terrible enemies tolerate each other if you ask them nicely.

Sagittarius Moon with **Scorpio Sun**

Your fascinations can turn into all-consuming obsessions, whether that's stamp collecting or gardening. You're popular and outgoing, with a love of travel and culture, and you're chatty about your interests. Emotionally, you're less easy to work out because you keep your fears and insecurities tightly zipped.

Sagittarius Moon with **Sagittarius Sun**

Fun-loving and full-on, you put all your energy into trying to understand the world around you. You enjoy people who have different views and beliefs to yours, but you still enjoy a good argument with them. Cheerful and good-natured, you love a challenge. You can be a bit of a risk-taker, too.

Sagittarius Moon with Capricorn Sun

You're a natural entrepreneur, amazing in business, with excellent connections. Your home life may need a bit of work, as you're rarely there, but surrounding yourself with a loving family is how you stay grounded. Your generous nature means you try to give everyone in your life a bit of your enthusiasm and goodwill.

Sagittarius Moon with Aquarius Sun

A charitable humanitarian, you know you can make a big difference in the world, and you see your own limitations as just a challenge to be overcome. The tougher things get, the more determined you become. You can be a little detached in your personal relationships, but you have a wide circle of weird and wonderful friends.

Sagittarius Moon with **Pisces Sun**

Philosophical and emotional, you feel deep compassion for the people close to you and want to help people who are not so well off. Clued up on the latest psychological theories, you want to know what makes people tick so you can build a better world for everyone.

MOON
IN
CAPRICORN

YOUR FIRST INSTINCTS

What's the responsible thing to do here?

When confronted with a new challenge, while your emotions are rising to the surface, your initial response is to ask yourself if you are being realistic. You're not a flapper, and you don't do drama — although if you're really excited about something, you may do a little dance of glee if nobody is looking. Your inner critic and sense of decorum forbid you to act rashly. You'll compose yourself, take a step back from the situation, and ask yourself what a responsible adult would do here. You exercise restraint and stay in control before the situation escalates. Once you have worked out how to come out the other side with your dignity intact, you'll make a practical plan and stick to it sensibly.

A study in self-reliance

Your emotional boundaries are clearly drawn, and you usually face emotional upsets quietly, on your own. Your self-sufficiency was probably learned in childhood, when you may have discovered that, sadly, spontaneous emotional outbursts were not appropriate or welcome. This is why you truly value the people in your life who have seen you at your most vulnerable or uncertain — they saw you vulnerable, scared or uncharacteristically thrilled, and didn't judge you — or even think to. You're the one usually placing yourself under strict rules, and the more you learn about why, the better. Knowing how you like to be comforted, and being able to express that to your loved ones, could be liberating.

WHAT YOU'RE ATTRACTED TO IN OTHERS

Cool high-achievers

A little cynical when it comes to love, you're not impressed with people who brag about their achievements or leave little to the imagination. But you find it attractive when you discover that someone you like is quietly successful. A little subtle name-dropping is fine by you, but posting terrible poetry on social media while scantily clad is not. Organized, practical types win you over by making you feel safe and secure, and if they're good with money, that also gets a big tick. You're a traditionalist and likely want a settled home and family life. At work you're a consummate professional, but your home needs to be a place where you can completely relax — so choosing someone with similar values will save any heartache further down the line.

The more perceptive, the better

You don't mind a little emotional neediness in a partner as long as it doesn't get too alarming and bubble up beyond your private life together. Denying your own feelings is a bad habit, so a partner who encourages you to look deeper inside yourself will intrigue. You're famous for burrowing into your career to escape icky emotions, so someone who can help bring you back to yourself will impress you with their perceptive insight. Little surprises you, or turns you on, more than someone who can see how you're really feeling. You can feel guilty when you ask the people you love for something you need emotionally, so when they already understand that about you, it helps.

YOUR FEARS AND EMOTIONAL RESPONSES

Failure

Your worst fear is that you'll not make it to the top of your mountain. You're the hardest worker in the zodiac, and have enviable stamina and determination to reach your goals. You usually calmly and sure-footedly find your way around obstacles, but occasionally you'll realize that your path is a dead end. You work incredibly hard to make it big, so you don't react well when life isn't fair or doesn't meet your expectations. You're not someone who gives up easily, and you have a habit of placing all your eggs in one basket, so when things don't work out you can get gloomy. Be careful you don't go blaming yourself for something that you could not save. Respect that you gave it your all, and that sometimes the result is out of your hands. Your happiness should not be entirely dependent on your professional successes.

Look on the bright side

Humour is how you stop yourself from losing your marbles. People who don't know you well can be taken aback by your clever wit and ridiculous black humour because you are usually such a serious, sensible person. Your ability to laugh at yourself keeps you sane when you're emotionally spent. You might be waist-deep in sorrow, rejected by a lover, penniless and watching mushrooms grow from your carpet, but you'll still be laughing at the hopelessness of it all. Humour is your therapy, whether you're poking fun at your own disasters or enjoying a great comedian. Humour keeps you from tipping into despair, and you love it for keeping you realistic when you get lofty ideas about what you might achieve.

WHAT YOU KEEP SECRET

Impostor syndrome

Even though there's oodles of evidence to the contrary, underneath your designer suit and impressive résumé you might feel like a fraud. It's hard for anyone to convince you otherwise, because deep down your confidence in yourself might be a little shaky. Status symbols like trophies, certificates, a fancy address or a Prada suit should be comforting, and remind you that you made it, but they rarely do much to convince you on an emotional level that you've achieved anything of value. You might ask yourself what it would take to make you feel like a winner, and whether the perfect job, house or relationship is what really matters — or whether a more altruistic or charitable goal could make you feel more fulfilled.

Can't open up

Because you find it awkward to share your feelings, and often feel it's your noble duty to keep your worries private, you bottle up your feelings. Intense emotions build pressure that eventually must be shared or channelled elsewhere. You might gallantly feel you don't wish to burden others with your problems, and try your best to ignore emotional gremlins, but you could be wonderfully surprised at how open the people around you will be when you spill the beans. Sometimes keeping yourself so tightly closed can give you an aloof edge. But admitting that you're human after all, to yourself and your loved ones, will only strengthen the bond between you and release you from your self-made shackles.

Sun and Moon combinations

Capricorn Moon with **Aries Sun**

You are ambitious, passionate and tough; your family and friends may think you're invincible. Probably a little highly strung, you need to relax and think before rushing in to save the day. Self-sufficient and quick-tempered, you prefer to be the leader or the main caretaker in your partnerships.

Capricorn Moon with **Taurus Sun**

Down-to-earth and capable, you are reliable, loyal and strong. You're a thoroughly sensible person with respect for the past, and you want to build a comfortable life for yourself and your loved ones. As patient as a saint in a dentist's waiting room, you take life slowly and have faith that it will all work out in the end.

Capricorn Moon with **Gemini Sun**

Tenacious but easily distracted, you chase your ambitions erratically but always reach your goals. Emotionally restless, you need variety and fun, and surround yourself with interesting people. You need a secure home life, and will value someone who recognizes when you need pulling out of your moody tendencies.

Capricorn Moon with **Cancer Sun**

Goal-oriented and good with money, you approach life cautiously and build your career slowly and carefully. You probably want your own family, as your home is where you are most yourself. At work you're the caring boss who looks after everyone, but you're still very ambitious.

Capricorn Moon with **Leo Sun**

You like being in the public eye, and as you're goal-focused and a great planner, you're skilled at putting on a show. Social and talented, you may have many admirers, but you crave a stable, close-knit home life with the people you love most.

Capricorn Moon with **Virgo Sun**

Methodical and organized, you can be quite strict with yourself about sticking to your routine. Good habits are the glue that holds you together, and you can see where others would benefit from doing the same. Quiet, kind and supportive, you're an excellent problem-solver and a brilliant researcher.

Capricorn Moon with **Libra Sun**

You're an elegant, graceful person with wonderful taste and good manners. Your judgment is sound, though it takes you a long time to come to conclusions. But when your mind is made up, you follow your path diligently. You need to worry less about what other people think, and focus on being you.

Capricorn Moon with **Scorpio Sun**

You're shrewd, ambitious and perceptive, though you may need a creative outlet to help you express your feelings more freely. You're extremely observant of the people around you, but you keep what you notice to yourself. Good communication skills will help you come out of your shell.

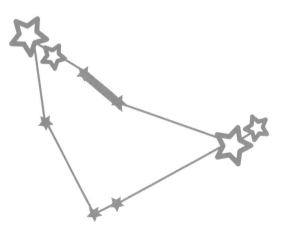

Capricorn Moon with Sagittarius Sun

Ambitious, serious-minded and responsible, you have a surprisingly brilliant sense of humour that helps you deal with life's absurdities. You can be competitive, as you love a challenge, and you usually play to win. Your confident public self hides a shy heart.

Capricorn Moon with Capricorn Sun

Quiet and wise, you don't like to steal the limelight, yet you're the person who always reaches their goals. You stick to your plans and set strict codes of conduct for yourself, and can get moody if you feel you've let yourself down. Your outrageous sense of humour serves as an essential emotional outlet.

Capricorn Moon with Aquarius Sun

You're an excellent businessperson who gets along with everyone at work. You enjoy sharing your interests with others and may be part of many groups and organizations. Remember to share your feelings, as you can be emotionally hard to read. Others may think you're aloof when you're just thinking about shoes.

Capricorn Moon with Pisces Sun

You're ambitious, with tremendous artistic and creative vision. Bringing your wonderful imagination to a bigger audience will help channel your empathy into making the world a better place. Your idealistic Sun is inspired by the common sense and stamina of your practical Moon sign, which gives you the power to turn dreams into reality.

MOON IN AQUARIUS

YOUR FIRST INSTINCTS

Detached and unselfish

You're the person who takes respected traditions and rebuilds them for the modern age. Dealing with your feelings can be uncomfortable, as you live in your head so much that when your emotions rise to the surface, you're not sure what's going on. You love being around people, and often think in terms of 'we' rather than looking out for yourself first. When heavy emotions move in, you become fascinated by how your friends and family cope with jealousy, grief, sudden feelings of attraction for your partner's brother, or rage at the destruction of the rainforests. By wanting to help the people around you first, you conveniently avoid facing your own issues while remaining a friendly and level-headed member of society.

How can I do this differently?

In moments of panic, sadness, anger or surprise, your autopilot mode alerts you to move away from what is expected of you. You seek to be an individual in all areas of your life, and your emotional responses are no exception. Forever free-spirited, you are extremely independent, which keeps you from doing the 'done' thing. Feeling categorized or patted into line makes you feel suffocated and brings out your rebellious nature. Emotions feel *animal*, and you're the humanitarian of the zodiac — the one who wants everyone to work together for a better planet. So seeing that your responses are irrational or out of control can be upsetting. Emotions seem to have their own secret rules, and you don't always know what they are.

WHAT YOU'RE ATTRACTED TO IN OTHERS

Unique qualities

One of the friendliest people around, you are profoundly curious about what makes others tick. Brilliant at finding fascinating or outrageous facts about everyone in your company, you home in on others' eccentricities and surprising stories. You know your mild-mannered uncle keeps it quiet that he was a fire-eater in the circus, or that your great aunt was one of the first women train drivers. Uncovering others' colourful stories is one of your loveliest traits, and it's what draws you to be their friend. In a romantic partner, you look for their unique qualities, but you're not overly interested in conventional good looks. It's the convention-smashers, tradition-changers and myth-squashers who really earn your admiration.

Mental stimulation

As you're sailing in uncharted waters, understanding the mysteries of emotional or sexual attraction is a lifelong challenge. You're fiercely independent, so committing yourself to a romantic relationship can be a tall order. Someone who can tickle you mentally will always get your attention, and clever types with something surprising to say will capture your imagination — and eventually, your heart. Always choosing the path less travelled, you're drawn to characters with alternative views and beliefs. You'll always have time for people who can convince you that humans have not scraped the surface of what they're capable of. People who believe time travel is possible, or that decoding dolphin squeaks could give profound insight to life's biggest mysteries, are your type.

YOUR FEARS AND EMOTIONAL RESPONSES

Being like everyone else

You fly as far away from ordinary as your Aquarian spaceship can carry you. The thought that you're just another brick in the wall gives you chills, and you'd rather be known for outrageous behaviour than for nothing of note. In your heart you're a revolutionary, so when you find yourself doing what most of your friends and acquaintances do — falling in love, eating three meals a day or picking out curtains with your partner — it makes you feel trapped. You want to be remembered for changing things, breaking the rules to make them more inclusive, saving the planet and campaigning for animal rights. You're the peace-loving revolutionary hippie campaigning for nuclear disarmament who uses your genius to come up with clean-energy solutions.

Emotional solace

If you're hurting, sad or feeling uncertain you find solace in becoming obsessed with anything from the Rubik's Cube to quantum physics. You're firmly in your comfort zone when you're learning a new skill, reading up on a curious scientific theory or working on how to trawl the sea for plastic. You'll also gather people around you when you're feeling out of sorts, because you like to be part of a group, team or club. Working on projects with other people helps you deal with feelings that need processing, so you won't have to discuss them or spend too much time analyzing them. Surrounding yourself with friendly faces helps you feel stable in troubled times.

WHAT YOU KEEP SECRET

Light years ahead

Because you think at lightning speed and can wrap your head excitedly around complex or esoteric ideas, you may get a little frustrated when others have difficulty getting into the same headspace, or when you have to slow down for them to catch up. Egalitarian to your core, your friendliness and comradeship impel you to include everyone in your plans and ideas — but it can be source of frustration when your brilliant ideas fall flat or are misunderstood. You understand obscure concepts that are beyond many, which can make you feel a little lonely. When you were much younger you probably learned that not everyone was on your wavelength, and sometimes not even on the same planet.

Intimacy is tricky

You're wonderfully friendly and warm with people you like, and you always find a way of forging a close mental connection. You're the master of making obscure references to things only the two of you have in common. This extra-thoughtful friendliness can be a little confusing to anyone who hopes to be more than just friends, as they might misinterpret this extra attentiveness as flirting. Weirdly, when you *are* attracted to someone, you try to avoid them, as you feel a little overwhelmed by your emotions and probably wouldn't feel comfortable getting that close. It's a confusing minefield, and you hope nobody realizes how exasperating it is for you to express your feelings.

Sun and Moon combinations

Aquarius Moon with **Aries Sun**

You want to make your mark on the world and will put tremendous effort into your passions. Independent and sometimes downright rebellious, you're at your best when you're fighting for a cause. Brilliant but impatient, you won't compromise on your humanitarian ideals.

Aquarius Moon with **Taurus Sun**

A stubborn mix of unchanging Taurus dependability and Aquarian curiosity, you make choices that are likely to be both groundbreaking and long-lasting. Your relationships are stable and loving, and you have a keen interest in different cultures. You enjoy the outside life and, although you enjoy home comforts, you also love being close to nature.

Aquarius Moon with **Gemini Sun**

You proudly march to the beat of a different drum. You are brilliantly versatile and clever, and your curious mind keeps you inventive, chatty and amusing. Your mind is constantly moving, and you have an insatiable appetite for knowledge, whether you're self-taught, highly educated or just skilled at squeezing information from friends.

Aquarius Moon with **Cancer Sun**

With a nurturing, emotionally intelligent Cancer Sun, you treasure family values and tradition, which are at odds with your restless, offbeat Aquarian Moon. You probably feel your friends are your family, and your love and loyalty mean you'll be the emotional compass at the centre of their lives.

Aquarius Moon with **Leo Sun**

Your creativity reaches every corner of your life, from your work to your relationships. If there's a way to make your world brighter or more interesting, you'll find it. Proud and broad-minded, you enjoy meeting people from different backgrounds and love to entertain.

Aquarius Moon with **Virgo Sun**

Helpful and brilliantly well-organized, you know how to make any plan or project a wild success. Amazing at solving puzzles, you never give up on your friends, and you remain loyal in the toughest of times. You're kind-hearted and open to new ideas, and you champion charitable causes.

Aquarius Moon with **Libra Sun**

An excellent judge of character, you take a while to make up your mind about people, but your fair and open-minded approach means you are surrounded by family and friends who look after you. You're both uber-practical and a hopeless romantic.

Aquarius Moon with **Scorpio Sun**

Resourceful and aloof, you're clever enough to find your way around any challenge or obstacle. Your Scorpio Sun means you have a sixth sense about the people you care about, and your friendly Aquarian Moon assures you have a close-knit bunch of interesting pals.

Aquarius Moon with **Sagittarius Sun**

Idealistic, open-minded and adventurous, you're one of life's explorers. Your open, exuberant, cheerful Sun works well with your clever, ever-logical Moon. Emotionally, you're one of a kind, memorable and quirky, and you're not afraid to take a gamble.

Aquarius Moon with **Capricorn Sun**

Your career-focused Capricorn Sun gives you the determination and stamina to reach any summit, while your idealistic, humanitarian Aquarian emotional side drives you to make life better for people who need it most. You've both the groundbreaking ideas and the staying power to make a huge difference.

Aquarius Moon with **Aquarius Sun**

Uniquely talented, you're extremely inventive and creative, and have the courage and energy to take boring or outdated traditions and ideas and re-make them entirely. Loved for your eccentric tastes and electric mind, you're a fabulous friend.

Aquarius Moon with **Pisces Sun**

Tuned into an unusual current, you have a compassionate, spiritual view of the world that colours your deep connections with the people around you. Your beliefs may be unusual, but your charisma and humanity draw open-minded, gentle people into your life who feel compelled to look after you.

MOON
IN
PISCES

YOUR FIRST INSTINCTS

Merge with the feeling

In moments of high emotional drama, your instinct is to either merge with what's happening or escape from it. You have the most sensitive, compassionate Moon sign of all, and sometimes your response to deep feelings of love, loneliness, joy or compassion is to dissolve your boundaries and be at one with the emotion on a pure level. You're more comfortable with feelings than you are with logical thinking, and deep down you know that the only way to understand your emotions is to experience them on a visceral level and let yourself swim in them. Dancing, swooning, sulking or screaming into a pillow may not be the most practical response, but you understand that experiencing your feelings is much healthier for you than not acknowledging them at all.

Escape artist

Because you feel the depths of human emotion so acutely — sometimes on a psychic level — you can become overwhelmed. Your capacity to empathize can be your best friend, but it can also make you want to check out on your own for a while. Your escapist Pisces Moon is associated with reading, fantasizing and partying if you're feeling pressurized… anything that makes the reality of your emotions less intense. Every now and then you need to be on your own to replenish your batteries and reconnect with the world beneath your feet, and your escape could be as simple as turning off your phone or taking a train to a place where nobody knows you and spending a day on the beach.

WHAT YOU'RE ATTRACTED TO IN OTHERS

Honest and practical

You can sometimes find it difficult to tell the difference between fact and fiction, fantasy and reality. So you need an honest anchor in your life, a true compass who can always point you in the right direction. You're drawn to practical, kind souls who deal with what's in front of them and encourage you to do the same. You can get lost in your own world, so having someone who gently pulls you back to life's necessities — like paying your mortgage, eating properly and having a sensible routine — will keep you rooted. You also deeply appreciate a person who can be honest with you without breaking you into a thousand pieces — tact and gentleness are very attractive character traits that you have yourself, but need just as much from your partner.

Firm boundaries

You need to learn to stick up for your own needs and desires, so if you know what's good for you, you'll look for someone who encourages you to be your own person. Instinctively, you'll want to merge with a partner, and will wish to understand them to the depths of their soul. But what you need is to take the more difficult task of working out who you are first. A true partner will help you define your boundaries while appreciating the creative and generous person you are. You need enough alone time to hear your own voice, and your other half will respect your need for solitude.

YOUR FEARS AND EMOTIONAL RESPONSES

Being misunderstood

Your introverted Pisces Moon brings a beautiful, but at times confusing, sea of turbulent feelings. Trying to describe how you feel or analyzing your feelings just seems to make them even more confusing, so you give up and let others draw their own conclusions. Bold, direct questions from others can be too on the nose, and make you squirm in their glare. How can you say how you feel when you're not that sure yourself? You fear that when you find it difficult to explain yourself clearly, you'll be judged harshly, or that others will invent their own stories when you can't give a clear account of your own.

Making sacrifices

You're a spiritual person who believes we are all connected, and that everybody's feelings and actions have a ripple effect. Your tireless generosity and compassion can be exhausting at times, but you have faith in a higher power and know that if you are good, kind and giving, the Universe will protect and defend you. Being willing to see the best in people whom others may have given up on, and proving to the people around you that love conquers all, is how you keep life's harsher, colder realities at bay.

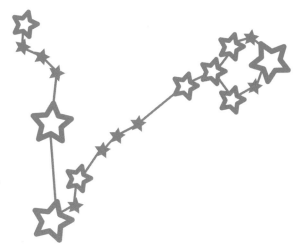

WHAT YOU KEEP SECRET

You know everyone else's secrets

Because you're so disarmingly open about your own inner life, other people feel able to share their most intimate thoughts. And perhaps because they sense your almost spiritual compassion, they may also confess to all sorts of mistakes or misdemeanours. You're also the most psychic sign of the zodiac, and your intuition is so hot that you usually know their secrets before they tell you. Knowing everyone else's secrets is an honour, but it can also be a burden you didn't ask for. You likely know the worst of what people are capable of as well as the noble things, but your forgiving nature means you gloss over the worst and shine your light on others' lovelier qualities.

You give it all away

One of the most wonderful things about you is that you trust people so easily, but you'll never admit how much of yourself you surrender to others. You rarely keep anything back for yourself; your life is an open book that you share with any waif or stray who connects with you. You'll cry in front of people you don't know, reveal your most intimate feelings to whoever's sat next to you on the bus, and hand out your credit card and PIN without ever expecting to be taken advantage of. So when your kindness is abused, it knocks you for six. You expect everyone to be as charitable and benevolent as you, and it can take you a long time to regain trust after you've been victimized. But you always do in the end because of your irrepressible faith in people.

Sun and Moon combinations

Pisces Moon with **Aries Sun**

Your sensitive Pisces Moon softens the impulsive, full-on energy of your Aries Sun. You're emotionally sensitive and compassionate, but when you decide to dedicate your time and energy to a cause, you're a force to be reckoned with. You're altruistic and passionate about helping others.

Pisces Moon with **Taurus Sun**

Serene and patient, you're a creative soul who views your world through a colourful lens and appreciates high-quality clothes and beautiful surroundings. Steady and loyal, you're a dependable, grounded person who has a sensual side and a big appetite for life's pleasures.

Pisces Moon with **Gemini Sun**

Your mind is rarely quiet, as you have an amazingly colourful imagination. Fiction writing should come naturally, as you have such a fertile fantasy life. Communicative and lively, you're never short of inspiring ideas, and you know exactly what to say when your friends need to hear inspiring words.

Pisces Moon with **Cancer Sun**

Deeply in tune with your loved ones' moods, you're so used to putting other people first that you forget your own needs and desires. You're a shy, private person who prefers to work alone, but enjoying a creative outlet helps you process your thoughts and feelings.

Pisces Moon with **Leo Sun**

Glamorous and mysterious, you exude an alluring, ethereal quality that hypnotizes others. Your Leo Sun means you're comfortable being the centre of attention, and your Pisces Moon ensures that you get along with people from all walks of life.

Pisces Moon with **Virgo Sun**

Modest and kind, you flip between your detail-obsessed Virgo Sun and your more chaotic, emotional Pisces Moon. One minute you're planning your meals for the week ahead, the next you're having a nap before a work deadline.

Pisces Moon with **Libra Sun**

You are compassionate, benevolent and fair-minded. Your Libra Sun dislikes being pressured into making decisions, because you always want to weigh up the evidence before judging. Your Pisces Moon is also very sensitive to discord and disharmony, which makes you a creative and sensitive soul.

Pisces Moon with **Scorpio Sun**

Your Pisces Moon may seem vague or directionless, but your Scorpio Sun usually knows exactly where it's going. You have reserves of emotional energy, and often have many different passions. You are distrustful of people you don't know, but you warm to them when they share their secrets.

Pisces Moon with **Sagittarius Sun**

Keenly interested in other people's beliefs, you probably enjoy travel and meeting people from different cultures. You can find it difficult to stick to a budget, and some financial-planning skills would stop you from being such an impulsive shopper!

Pisces Moon with **Capricorn Sun**

An alluring mix of quiet determination and emotional intelligence, you take life quite seriously. But you have an off-the-wall sense of humour even in the most challenging circumstances, and brilliant intuition when it comes to earning money.

Pisces Moon with **Aquarius Sun**

Your tech-savvy Aquarius Sun has you tuned into the zeitgeist, and you'll be years ahead of your time in some way. You're something of a maverick — sometimes extremely empathic, sensitive and caring, but also erratic, contrary and a little aloof.

Pisces Moon with **Pisces Sun**

You feel linked to a mysterious world of impressions and emotions that other people aren't even aware of, but your chameleon-like character helps you adapt to other people and changing circumstances. Keep some of your kindness and energy for yourself.